INIE -

a life of mission and prayer

by Eileen John Austin ocd

Contents

		Page
Introduction	. . . .	1
1. A curate's daughter	. . . . . .	5
2. Nine little orphans	. . . . .	9
3. Aunt Lily	. . . .	12
4. Confirmation	. . . .	16
5. Growing up	. . . .	20
6. The missionary vocation	. . . . .	23
7. China	. . . .	29
8. Kien Ning	. . . .	38
9. New horizons	. . . . . .	43
10. Hessie	. . . .	50
11. Captain Newcombe	. . . . .	64
12. Yokohama	. . . .	72
13. Tokyo and Kozuke District Officer	. . .	78
14. Taking Lucy's place	. . . . .	86
15. China? Not yet	. . . . .	91
16. Two more years in China	. . . .	97

17.   Fourteen years of struggle   105

18.   More to come   115

19.   The Welsh Mission   118

20.   Sister Mary of Jesus   130

21.   Novitiate days   140

22.   Holy Year 1933.   147

23.   1934-1935   151

24.   The last year   156

Epilogue   162

Introduction

Writing the life-story of a Carmelite nun means mapping out a long journey. For a vocation is just what the name implies – a call from God. It begins with the call into existence when the eternal idea God conceived of each person finds expression in time: a child is born and through many experiences, God reveals his plan and his abiding love for that person.

Every Carmelite can look back and perceive with hindsight that her early years before entering an enclosed order were a preparation for a life of union with God's salvific love. Many and varied experiences introduce the future Carmelite to the world's great need for intercessors; and once inside the cloister, the world comes knocking at her door asking for prayers.

Recently a well-known Cancer Care charity, which collects used stamps, expressed amazement at the number and variety of the foreign stamps sent in regularly by one community (even after the advent of e-mail). And, quite apart from letters, each Sister sponsors by prayer and sacrifice her own special worldwide concerns as the Holy Spirit moves her. She seeks by her communion with her Saviour to become 'Love in the Heart of the Church'. This was how Saint Therese of Lisieux saw her vocation, but she realized that her life in Carmel was only a dress rehearsal for her true mission of prayer for the world from her place in heaven.

The life-story that will be unfolded in these pages is no different from any of our lives – each is a love-story between the Creator and the work of his hands fashioned in the likeness of the beloved Son's humanity. If the life of Inie Newcombe was adventurous during her years in China and Japan, it was also very ordinary for the greater part of her childhood and later years. She spent her last five years as an enclosed nun hidden away in the wilds of North Wales until her death in

1936.

After ten years had elapsed, her community was persuaded to write a short biography, drawing on her own account of her conversion. This was published in 1951 by the Catholic Truth Society under the title 'At the Eleventh Hour' – a most unfortunate title, as it gave the impression that her life until she became a Carmelite had not been 'working in the Lord's vineyard'!

This pamphlet was circulated to many Carmelite communities and perhaps a little further, but over the years it fell into oblivion and the publishers in 1991 could find no record of it. Most probably it was, in its final form, written at the suggestion of Fr. Michael Egan SJ, who was Superior of the Jesuit house in Leeson Street, Dublin from 1922, and was Inie's friend and director after her conversion, the story of which he encouraged her to write. He died in 1961 at the age of 86 and is even now remembered by the Sacred Heart Sisters in Dublin - 'an absolute character, full of fun and humour, and famous for his outrageously funny verses, written rather at the expense of the nuns but never giving offence'.

Since 1992, there had been renewed interest in the life of Inie Newcombe. It began with the discovery of a wooden box of picture postcards dating back to the foundation of the Carmelite monastery at Dolgellau where Inie ended her life. Right at the bottom was a small album of faded photographs of the San Yong mission in China at the turn of the century, including one of 'Miss Newcombe's Residence'.

This discovery led to an enquiry being sent to the Church Missionary Society of the Church of England. They gave permission for research into their archives, which had been transferred to the Birmingham University Library. This produced very interesting information, not only about the seven years Inie spent in China, but also about her three sisters who were there from 1886 to 1913. A fellow missionary had compiled notes about the family in view of an obituary notice. This aroused much interest, and the two surviving members of the community who had lived with Inie after she became a Carmelite, wrote down all they could remember about her and the stories she told about her childhood and missionary years. Some of her letters were also found. These revealed the story of her extraordinary vocation as a Carmelite at the age of seventy-four. A later enquiry brought an abundance of information from the Salvation Army about her years in Japan. Thanks are also due to the Church of Ireland archives for information about the father and brother of Inie, who were clergymen. Since then more information has been found from old accounts of the Fukian mission and the Hwa Sang massacre.

The diocese of Armagh of the Church of Ireland was the soil in which God planted a seed called Inie, which was to bear fruit for His glory and the spread of His Kingdom.

4

# A Curate's daughter

In the year of Our Lord 1850 a newly-ordained minister of the Established Church of Ireland left his Dublin home and Trinity College to take up his first post as curate at Pomeroy, Co. Tyrone, near Omagh. He was Benjamin Arthur Newcombe, son of the Dublin merchant who had built Newcombe Bridge across the Liffey. Three years after his ordination, the young curate married his third cousin Elizabeth Maria Frances Wilhelmina Eccles.

It seems to have been the custom to give several forenames, very often including William, Mary and Elizabeth, in homage to those good Protestant monarchs, and also to differentiate between the many Eccles cousins. The boys were often given the surnames of their grandparents as forenames. Thus Rev. Newcombe was Benjamin Braddel Arthur in the clergy lists of his diocese. His third child born at Pomeroy followed his father into the ministry, and so we know that his full name was John Dickson Eccles Newcombe. The young couple named their first child William and their second Jemima with some additions, but the little girl was soon known as Mina[1]. Her mother was known to the cousins as Aunt Inie[2].

In 1857 Rev. Newcombe was given charge of St. Mark's, Drogheda, a chapel-of-ease of the main church of St Peter's. St Mark's had been built in 1828 to accommodate the families who could not find room for a family pew in St Peter's. The living at the time was about £98 per annum, and here the Newcombe family settled until 1862.

In 1857 on August 5th Mrs. Newcombe gave birth to her second daughter, the heroine of this story, and named her Elizabeth. She was always known as Inie, like her mother, and so one of her names was probably Wilhelmina, but she would never admit the fact and her baptismal entry at Drogheda was not found. Actually there is no record of her father baptizing any of his four daughters born at Drogheda, so perhaps he was not over-zealous when it came to keeping the records. Suffice to say that in her old age, Inie insisted that her Catholic baptism was only conditional because…'I was baptized by my father and he was a clergyman and knew how to baptize.'[3]

After Inie came Maude in 1859, Lucy in 1860 and Hessie or Hester in 1862. Lucy was crippled from birth or early childhood, cared for by her brothers and sisters, but later herself supported their active service of God's Kingdom by her prayers. The curate of St Peter's at this time was Rev. John Eccles, five years older than Rev. Newcombe and a fellow student at Trinity College. He might even have been his brother-in-law, although there were many Eccles cousins – Mrs. Newcombe's father was a Justice of the Peace of Ecclesville, Co. Tyrone.

In 1862 Rev. Newcombe moved to another parish in Co.Tyrone, close to Pomeroy, although still in the diocese of Armagh. Inie remembered being told that he volunteered to go farther north to support the Protestant cause in an area where the Catholics were in the majority. He moved his family of seven children to Donaghmore Upper and took charge as Perpetual Curate of the Church of St Patrick, built in 1842 and cut off from the main parish in 1843. There were in the parish 3,000 Protestants and about 5,000 Catholics with three RC chapels.

Inie would have been a little girl of five at the time, and would have absorbed the strict separation that existed between Protestants and the native Catholics. There was also a divide between rich and poor, which coincided with the religious dichotomy. The Romish superstition was 'the religion of servants and bog-people', though by 1862, although still poor, it was producing new churches everywhere, as well as schools and colleges.

But the Holy Spirit knows no such boundaries and Inie grew up in a deeply religious environment. She and her little brothers and sisters were soon to go through a time of testing and their faith and trust in God's love would come out victorious, thanks to their parents' example.

Soon after the move to Donaghmore Upper news came to them that the Vicar of Drogheda, Rev. Edward Kelly, had died. He was only 58. This sad news was soon followed by happier tidings when the little Newcombe children learned from their father that their friend Rev. John Eccles had been made Vicar of Drogheda. Their father had been replaced at St Mark's by Rev. John Monsarratt who had just come back from ten years chaplaining in Gambia, West Africa. He also was well known to Rev. Newcombe since they had both gained their B.A. in 1847 at Trinity College.

Probably the children had left their hearts in Drogheda where the four little girls had been born. There had been holidays by the sea and visits from grandparents. At Donaghmore they never really settled. Their mother was occupied with the new baby, Charles Thomas, born about 1863, and their father with his sermons. They were very proud of him, and as Inie was to write in her old age 'In the Protestant service, given a spiritual clergyman and a devout congregation, well-chosen hymns and a good choir, you have it at its best and it goes far: I have been deeply moved and spiritually uplifted at such services'.

Scarcely eighteen months after their arrival at Donaghmore their father became ill and after a few weeks without any sign of improvement, he had to make the painful decision to resign. This meant, of course, that they had to move again, since a new curate was appointed. A house belonging to the family was vacant in Kingstown, the port of Dublin, and this was made ready for them by friends and relatives.

So, in the summer months, the children were packed into a coach with their trunks and provisions, and set off on the long journey south, while their parents followed at a slower pace, with many stops for the sick man to rest. Mrs. Newcombe was at this time expecting another baby. They put their trust in

8

God's loving protection, but it was a very anxious time for the parents and they were thankful to arrive at Dublin.

 Nine little orphans[4]

The months that followed the arrival of the family at Kingstown (modern Dun Loughaire), remained blurred in the memories of the children. In later life, they could only remember the facts – the events that turned their young lives upside-down. The journey from the north had been too much for their father, already ill, and his condition worsened as the summer wore to its close. The children spent much time away from the house so as not to disturb him. They would often have sat on the pier with their nursemaid, watching the steamers and sailing ships. The word soon went round 'Those are the Newcombe children – poor dears – their father is dying – only thirty nine – such a pity – their poor mother'.

The three eldest, William at ten, Mina nine, John eight, felt their father's illness most. They had always been proud of him, loved to hear him preach and loved him no less when he was strict with them. Sitting on the pier, they talked quietly and became older and wiser.

Inie, at seven, must have felt isolated, neither old enough to join them yet somehow no longer a little girl. All that was expected of her was to play with her little sisters and be a good girl. She remembered being corrected for her quick temper, which would spark out quite often. She learnt to control it when it was pointed out to her that she might hurt her little crippled sister, Lucy. She always had an exceptional memory and a gift for story telling, and that was probably used to lighten those dark days for the children.

When autumn arrived, it became all too clear that God was calling their father home. The feelings of his sorrowing wife and children could best be expressed in the words of a hymn in the new hymnbook, 'Hymns Ancient and Modern', which had been published four years previously:

Christ will gather in His own
To the place where He is gone,
Where their heart and treasure lie,
Where our life is hid on high.

Day by day the voice saith, 'Come,
Enter thine eternal home,'
Asking not if we can spare
This dear soul it summons there.

Had he asked us, well we know,
We should cry, 'O spare this blow!'
Yes, with streaming tears should pray,
'Lord, we love him, let him stay'.

But the Lord doth nought amiss
And since He hath ordered this,
We have nought to do but still
Rest in silence on His will.

Many a heart no longer here
Ah! Was all too inly dear
Yet, O Love, 'tis Thou dost call
Thou wilt be our All in all. Amen.

Eight little children sat in a row at their father's funeral. Uncles and aunts talked to them in the days that followed about heaven and Mama tried to cheer them with the news that God was going to send them a new baby after Christmas. She needed all her courage and faith, and her friends rallied round her to ease her burden. The children would have had many invitations to Christmas parties, which they tried to enjoy.

But as New Year 1865 approached and Mrs. Newcombe prepared for her confinement, it was clear that all was not well and the birth of a baby girl on January 9th was attended by complications. Within a fortnight, the mother was at death's door and had to accept God's call to entrust her nine children to His care. She asked the friend who was nursing her: 'Bring me my Bible and we shall see what the Lord will say to us'. She opened the Bible and the first text which caught her eye was: 'He is a Father of the fatherless' (Ps 68:5) – and from that moment the poor mother ceased to worry and died peacefully.

But the big question had to be solved: what was going to happen to the nine young children?

Evidently a wet-nurse had been found for the baby, whom her mother had named Benjamina after her father. The friend who had taken over during these tragic weeks sent telegrams to the relatives begging them to take two or three of the children into their homes. God did not delay in rewarding the dying mother's faith in His Providence.

3 Aunt Lily[5]

Among the aunts and uncles of the Newcombe children was one who was probably considered least likely to prove a good choice as foster-mother. Elizabeth Maria Newcombe, called Aunt Lily by her nephews and nieces lived quite near in Black-rock, at 25, Merrion Avenue, and she had the whole house to herself. But against this one advantage, one had to weigh the facts. She was single, had never dealt with children – at least not in such quantities, and worst of all, she was a Dissenter. Aunt Lily had opted out of the Established Church and joined the Ply-mouth Brethren. She spent one hour every day in prayer, and gossip averred that she was trying to be a nun.

25 Merrion Avenue, Blackrock. Co. Dublin

Aunt Lily's house

However, any-one who prays well and sincerely 'Thy Kingdom come, Thy will be done' puts them-selves at God's disposal. Aunt Lily realized when the telegram arrived that the ball was in her court, and that God was asking her to sacrifice her quiet life.

She was probably the eldest of the family and already middle-aged, for in 1897, thirty-two years later, Inie wrote of her, 'my aunt is already old and feeble'. So she said her Fiat and got on the bus to Kingstown.

One would like to have been there when she made her offer to take all nine children to her home! All we know is what was passed on to the children and recorded for posterity by Inie in her old age:

When Aunt Lily arrived and saw the children, she said, 'This family must *not* be divided', and she took all nine. She promised to take complete charge of them and all that concerned their future.

She also promised to bring them up in their father's religion.

The children recognized a really loving heart and responded gratefully. They set about packing their clothes and treasures and Aunt Lily ordered cabs and wagons for the next day, for their beds and cots would be needed. We can imagine her breaking the news to her cook and housemaid on her return – the alarm and 'Glory be to God' etc. Aunt Lily told them there was nothing to worry about as regards financing the venture, since each child had been provided for in their father's will with a yearly allowance from safe investments.

Rumours must have flown round Blackrock as supplies were laid in and Cook's explanation of the situation must have caused many a tear and prayer: 'God bless the good woman!'

Soon the cabs arrived from Kingstown full of shy children to be shown round their new home; and home it was to be. Aunt Lily loved the children and they knew it and responded with love. She made a truly happy home for them and taught them by word and example to be kind and unselfish with each other. There was at last a feeling of permanence and security. We have to remember that the two eldest had moved house three times. Even the baby, who was probably still living with her nurse, would have moved twice. The last six months at Kingstown were better forgotten, but Aunt always kept alive the children's memories of their parents and a real veneration for them. 'They were in heaven with God and God was very near in that house'.

Inie tells us:

> I was brought up in a deeply religious atmosphere, and my earliest memories are of spasmodic concerns over questions relating to conversion and personal religion. My aunt and guardian, the only parent I remember, was one of the most markedly religious women I have ever met. Her life was one of whole-hearted devotion to God. Every day shortly after breakfast, she retired to her room and spent an hour alone with God. Nothing was allowed to interfere with this. Visitors to the house, callers, no matter how urgent, must wait: orders were explicit: she must not be disturbed. Her chief duty she considered was the charge she had undertaken of her brother's nine orphan children. She often explained to us that she looked on this charge as a life-work given her by God Himself. Hers was real religion lived out in the details of everyday life before us children, and it is to her I owe the strong hold God has had on my whole life.

Part of school holidays were spent in the country and the older children were expected to take care of little crippled Lucy and see she was never left out of anything. At their own expense, they would hire a donkey or pony to take her with them, one of the boys staying with her. Mina, of course, was quite used to being nursemaid to successive toddlers.

'Our Aunt' thought of everything! She had a relative, a clergyman of the Church of Ireland (it had been dis-established in 1869) who had ten sons. The Newcombe boys, William, John and Charles, were sent to stay with him every year for a holiday, to experience a perhaps needed discipline at the hands of someone accustomed to the needs of boys. Needless to say, they enjoyed it!

Each child's bank account was kept separately, and if one needed more, as for instance Lucy did, Aunt Lily would pay the extra herself. When each one reached his or her twenty-first birthday, the new 'grown-up' received a chequebook and their share of the legacy.

 # Confirmation

As soon as the Newcombe children were settled in their new and permanent home with Aunt Lily at Blackrock, arrangements were made for them to attend Sunday services at the parish church of St Philip and St James, Booterstown, situated in Mount Merrion Avenue[6]. It was about a ten-minute walk passing perhaps the Dominican Convent of Sion Hill, of which more later. Soon the question of Confirmation arose for William and Mina, who, in 1867.

would have been fourteen and thirteen years of age. This entailed staying behind after evensong, for a more intense study of the cate-chism.

St Philip and St James, the church attended by the nine orphans

Although the official teach-ing of the Protestant re-ligion was that there were only two Sacraments instituted by Christ and necessary for salvation, Baptism and Eucharist, nevertheless the other five were retained in the established Church, and Confirmation was a very important stage in a child's life. By it, the young person freely declared his or her intention to live up to the promises made at Baptism.

The Bishop came on the day appointed and solemnly asked the candidates: 'Do you here, in the presence of God, and of this congregation, renew the solemn promise and vow that was made in your name at your Baptism, ratifying it and confirming the same in your own persons, and acknowledging yourselves bound to believe and do all those things which your God-parents then undertook for you?' They all answer, 'I do'. Then the Bishop lays his hands on the head of each one kneeling before him, saying, 'Defend, O Lord, this Thy child with Thy heavenly grace that he may continue Thine forever and daily increase in Thy holy Spirit more and more until he come unto Thy everlasting Kingdom'.

After Confirmation the young person was allowed to receive Holy Communion on Sunday and Holy days. Since John and Inie had scarcely the difference of a year between their ages, they were probably confirmed together in 1870. For John this was a step on the way to following in his father's footsteps. In a few years he would begin his studies for ordination at Trinity College. But for Inie it caused a major crisis in her spiritual journey. She tells us[7]:

> I was brought up a member of the established Church of which my father was a minister. We were carefully instructed in what was called the Romish Controversy: all my teachers agreed there. But on all other points there were contradictory views in a bewildering variety, the holders of which were always ready to dogmatise on the truth as they happened to hold it. And so, though I sorely needed spiritual help, I had no courage to seek it there.

> When I was about fourteen, I attended a set of classes preparatory to Confirmation, and my spiritual perplexity and fears increased. I found myself faced with duties and responsibilities with regard to God that I felt utterly unable to fulfil, and yet I could not escape, for to refuse Confirmation, I was told, was equal to refusing God, deliberately turning away from Him. That I would not do – and so I was confirmed. As we stood to sing the closing hymn "O Jesus, I have promised to serve Thee to the end," a

sense of crushing helplessness swept over me. I whispered a prayer: "I have promised, Lord, but I can't do it. However, I know that if I ever find out how, I will." At once a feeling of peace crept into my heart, and I know God heard and accepted my promise, and that sometime light would come.

Light was already dawning for Inie as she clung to the words of that hymn:

O Jesus, I have promised to serve Thee to the end.
Be Thou forever near me, my Master and my Friend.
I shall not fear the battle if Thou art by my side,
Nor wander from the pathway if Thou wilt be my guide.

She was to say in her old age after many battles and dark nights of searching: 'The one desire of my heart was to live wholly and entirely for God'[8]. In this she had a wonderful example in her aunt, and one can imagine that there were many abortive attempts to emulate Aunt's hour of prayer. There was also a constant reminder of a life consecrated to God in the fact that the back bedroom windows of No 25 overlooked the

Dominican Convent School on Merrion Avenue

grounds of a convent of nuns. Although the convent and school was quite a long way from No 25 (about twenty houses away on the same side), the girls' playing fields extended behind the houses all the way from the convent to the coast road. Beyond the playing fields was a path called by the nuns 'St. Catherine's Avenue', and it was there that Inie could see the nuns walking up and down.

The Dominican nuns first came to Ireland in 1644[9], when a convent was founded in Galway. But by 1714 the Penal Laws had cruelly disrupted the religious and apostolic life of the community, and they were evicted and driven into hiding. The Father Provincial managed to persuade the Archbishop of Dublin, Very Rev. Doctor Edward Byrne, to receive them into his diocese, where the Penal Laws were less strictly enforced, and in 1717 they were once again able to live as a community in a former Benedictine monastery. Some years later they moved to an estate on the north side of Dublin known as Cabra, and are still known at home and on the missions as the Cabra Dominicans.

In 1836 a group of Sisters from Cabra founded a convent and school near Blackrock in an area known as Mount Sion. They were enclosed nuns going out only to teach in the school. They rose at 5.30 am and sang the full Divine Office in choir, keeping silence apart from teaching and one recreation which they usually spent out-of-doors walking along St. Catherine's Avenue.

No 25 was to be Inie's home for twenty-one years, so she must have watched the nuns many times in their white habits and black veils and cloaks. But it did nothing to crack the hard shell of anti-Catholicism that had encased her and her milieu since early childhood. Nevertheless a seed was sown, and she was to say later in life, 'The idea of a convent life in general has always appealed to me from my childhood, when from my bedroom window I overlooked the enclosure of a Dominican convent, and saw the Sisters pacing up and down.[10]' However, a vast gulf separated her from that vocation, for she admits[11] that she personally added to the Thirty-nine Articles her own fortieth article, namely, that the Church of Rome was the Sink of Iniquity. It was the religion of servants and bog-people, and quite infra dig. It would be many more years before she actually met a Catholic in friendly conversation, and that would happen far away in China.

5   Growing up

W hen Aunt Lily first took charge of her nine little orphans, their ages ranged from a few months to twelve years. But the years passed. We know little about their early schooling but soon enough they began to leave the nest for one reason or another, leaving Aunt some oases of peace, although they were always sure of a welcome home. The three boys spent their holidays with their clergyman uncle and his large family of boys. Soon enough William and John became Trinity College scholars[12] and probably weekly boarders. Charlie followed them in 1879. John already had his B.A. in 1877 and began his studies for ordination. William came of age in 1874 and was the first to receive his chequebook and his allowance left by his father, which amounted to about forty pounds per annum. He emigrated to Canada, the same year and set up as a merchant in Ontario. In 1875 he married Ellen Atkinson, daughter of a clergyman from Limerick who had emigrated to Canada when Ellen was four years old. They settled at Fort William, a small town on the shores of Lake Superior, where William was the lighthouse keeper and local magistrate. The town, later named Thunder Bay, must have been home to many Irish Protestant families for he became Founder Master of the Orange Lodge.

About 1877, when Inie was twenty[13], she went on a grand tour of Europe with her elder sister, and had a short but significant encounter with a Roman Catholic. They were in Florence, two plainly-dressed 'English' ladies, for the girls had joined the Holiness Movement of Mr. Pigott. A man stopped them in the street and asked Inie the time in English. He explained that he knew no other language and had guessed from their appearance that they were English. Before Inie could answer, Mina cried out in alarm, pulling her away. 'He's a Romish priest, Inie; can't you see? Come away! Come away!' Inie, however, seems to have been brave enough to stand her ground for as long as it took her to say, 'It's half-past two' (or whatever it was), and in that moment, the monster took out a small crucifix and begged her to accept it. Inie was all for keeping it, and so Popish an emblem does not appear to have unduly upset her. But her sister frowned on impiety so outrageous. Since it was causing friction between them, Inie tried to get rid of it, putting it out of sight in trunk or box, only to find it turning up again and again like the proverbial bad penny, until finally she gave up trying to hide it. It was the humble prototype of the Carmelite profession cross she was one day to wear over her heart. But at this stage the incident made no difference, and the seed would lie buried for many more years.

Doubtless the family supported any charitable collection in aid of the starving poor during the second outbreak of the Potato Famine which raged in Ireland at the time. But it did little to disturb the peace of their middle-class existence. Possibly the alleged appearance of the Virgin Mary at Knock and the Land League which united the starving tenant farmers in protest against the landlord system was discussed with disapproval.

Of more interest to the family was the great day of John's ordination at Meath in 1880, and his first appointment as curate at Ardbraccan. There would have been much knitting of black socks and pullovers for the new Reverend Newcombe. Great was the joy when, in 1881, he was appointed curate of the nearby church on Carysfort Road for three years.

When Maude was old enough she asked to train as a nurse at the Rotunda Hospital, Dublin. She was clever and capable, although rather plain. She had made up her mind quite young to be a missionary and thought nursing would be useful, and qualified in midwifery. Hessie had suffered from eye trouble, and was often obliged to spend hours in a darkened room. Once, when alone and praying in the dark, she felt that God came to her and spoke to her, and the joy was almost unbearable. This was the Tabor, which prepared her for her Calvary some fifteen years later, when she died for her faith in China at the hands of the Boxers, aged, like her Saviour, thirty-three years.

As for Benjamina, we are indebted to a fellow-missionary, Flora Codrington, for an account of her school days, which adds colour to this period of the story of the family.

Benjamina seems to have been altogether charming, never spoilt, good-looking, clever, witty and sweet-tempered. When she was fifteen (1880), she went as a weekly boarder to Miss Taylor's school at Blackrock, where she was most popular. Aunt Lily had no taste in dress, and poor Bennie was a sight in utterly unsuitable clothes, but such things never worried her; she was full of fun. She wished very much to learn drawing, but Aunt Lily had a theory that it would make her eyes crooked, so would not allow it. She was a very good pianist, but had absolutely no ear, yet she could master any piece; nothing was too difficult for her. At home she was called Beanie, at school Bennie, and in China 'Benso'.

A very important event in the life of the family was the marriage of Reverend John to his cousin Mina, or Jemima Eccles. The date is uncertain, but probably the wedding took place before he was appointed Rector of Monasteroris in 1883. They do not seem to have had any children, but a sister-in-law was as good as a sister, and the fact that she had become an auxiliary member of the CEZMS, the Church of England Zenana Mission Society, was to contribute to the missionary vocations of her sisters-in-law, as we shall see. Jemima outlived her husband, and was probably one of the Eccles cousins with whom Mina went to live at 37 Grosvenor Road, Rathgar.

Jemima died in 1945 at a good old age.

 The missionary vocation

In her old age, Inie was described by Fr. Michael Egan as 'a plump, cheerful little body, the sort of person it does you good to meet'. That description would probably have fitted the young Inie in her early twenties. But her spiritual life was far from stable. She was a seeker and had not yet found. That one desire of hers to live entirely for God so often met with failure. Most of us go through a period of spiritual highs and lows alternating until we realize that faith must grow up and learn not to depend on feelings of fervour; to be grateful when they are there, but if not, to soldier on behind our banner the Cross. Inie did just that and describes the break-through to spiritual maturity thus[14]:

> Outwardly all seemed right but inwardly all was unstable. There would be a few weeks effort to find peace after attending special Missions followed by failure and long intervals of despair. I had lost confidence in religious teachers and I asked counsel of none.
>
> When I was about twenty-five another crisis came, and again turning away from man's help, I prayed with tears for light: and it came. An interior voice, without sound, flashed a clear message, and, in a moment, I realized that my Saviour was offering to undertake Himself the work of my sanctification. And, with as complete a surrender as I was capable of, I gave myself over into His hands, to do with me what He willed. Deep peace took possession of my heart and a glad free life opened out for me.

Now Inie was ready for the call to follow her Saviour to

the ends of the earth. But it was a family affair, and possibly Maude was the first to experience the call. As we have seen, she enrolled as a student nurse to equip herself for her missionary vocation.

This was the period of history which saw a slow but determined revolution in the status of women in Europe. When Victoria came to the throne at the age of eighteen, women were denied higher education, let alone the vote; universities and the legal and medical professions were closed to them; there were no trained nurses. These occupations were considered 'un-ladylike'. But as Victoria made it clear that she intended to rule, women set out to claim their rights. As early as 1870, Suffrage Societies were being formed although women did not get the vote until 1918. The first women doctors had to study abroad and the first women to attend university lectures were often accompanied by a chaperone.

The Church Missionary Society, founded in the eighteenth century, was all male apart from wives and sisters. But the women of India could not be evangelized by men, forbidden as they were by strict laws of purdah to have any contact with men other than those of their own household. They lived in a world of their own, bringing up their children in the women's quarters or 'zenana'. In 1880 the CMS decided to found the CEZMS - the Church of England Zenana Missionary Society - to train single women to bring the Gospel to the women of India. Women all over Britain formed support groups to raise funds for the venture. One such group was formed in Dublin around 1883 and Jemima Newcombe, Inie's sister-in-law soon got the family involved with fund-raising. An annual report was circulated by the new society and a bulletin entitled 'Women of India'.

But God was not calling the Newcombe sisters to India. About this time[15] Providence arranged that Robert W. Stewart, a young Dublin CMS missionary was sent to Foochow, one of the Treaty Ports in the Fuhkien province of China (Fujian in the modern romanization) He saw there the same need for women missionaries as in India since Chinese women had little freedom outside their homes. The new society arranged for Miss Gough, the daughter of a missionary in Ning Po to travel south and help at Foochow. In spite of having to learn a new dialect she was able to start a class for little boys in the morning and one for women in the afternoon. But after only three years she married and returned to Ning Po. Now in 1885 Rev. Stewart took home-leave and spoke to the Dublin group of CEZ auxiliaries about the need for volunteers for China and in particular his own need in Foochow.

His appeal did not fall on deaf ears and all four Newcombe girls felt the Lord was calling them. Inie, of course, had no hesitation and her enthusiasm carried the day with Aunt Lily. She was twenty-eight and well able to look after herself. Maude had to finish her nursing and midwifery first and Benjamina was not yet twenty-one and knew she had to wait. Hessie also longed to go but said nothing, thinking of the sorrow it would cause Aunt Lily. If all four of them left home it would leave all the care of the home and dear crippled Lucy to Mina and Aunt, now in her late sixties. But one day, to her surprise and delight, Aunt turned to her quite suddenly and asked, 'Do you want to be a missionary too?' Hessie owned up that it was the dream of her life. Aunt immediately made arrangements and the Candidates' secretary, Mrs. Sandys, was delighted to hear that a fourth recruit for China was asking to be accepted for training. Besides Inie and Hessie, two other ladies had answered the call from Dublin: Miss C. Bradshaw and Miss Davies.

The course for candidates was given in London at a house called 'The Willows' where they lived together and practised the lessons of cooking and house-keeping which were given. Aunt Lily had seen to it that her nieces were well trained in domestic science but there was also instruction in biblical and religious subjects, history of the missions, languages and culture, and the problems of work and health in tropical climates. Some medical instruction was given at Bethnal Green Mission Hospital. There were ten ladies in the September 1885 course and at the end Inie and Hessie were accepted to sail the following Spring to begin their probation and study of Chinese at Foochow, the port and capital of Fuhkien province.

Christmas 1885 must have been the last time the whole family were re-united. William would surely have come from Canada when he heard that four of his sisters were going to the Far East. John would have to take the Morning Service at Monasteroris but he and Jemima would have joined them in the afternoon. A few weeks later there was Benjamina's twenty-first birthday to celebrate, the last of them to come of age. Then Inie and Hessie returned to The Willows, Charlie to Trinity College and Maude to her nursing.

The following excerpts from the Candidates Committee give the bare bones of those years when Aunt Lily's brood spread their wings and left the nest.

10th March 1885: Ten names of ladies provisionally accepted as probationers include Misses I. & H. Newcombe. The September class consisted of fourteen ladies.

29th March 1886: Ladies hoping to sail include the Misses Newcombe.

8th Sept. 1887: The sub-committee considered the offer of Miss Maude Newcombe, sister of our Foochow missionaries, and resolved that, subject to the usual formalities, she be admitted to The Willows as a probationer with a view to training.

7th Dec. 1837: After the three months course it was recommended that she be accepted for training.

4th April 1888: Recommended that Miss M. Newcombe serve in Shanghae.

16th July 1888: It was recommended that Miss Benjamina Newcombe be accepted to go forth at her own charges in the autumn and that she and her sister Maude proceed together to Shanghae to commence work there on the specific fund kindly granted by an anonymous donor for this purpose.

Benjamina was only twenty-three when she sailed for China, apparently without going through the training course. There was some urgency to begin the work and Maude needed a companion. The CEZMS had had to refuse earlier pleas from China on the grounds of lack of funds and personnel. So understandably they viewed these four sisters as a gift from God, especially as they all refused to draw a salary apart from board and lodging, each of them having an allowance of between 40 and 60 pounds a year.

28

Map of Fuh-kien Province, the size of England, with population of 20,000,000

CEZMS Stations are indicated by +

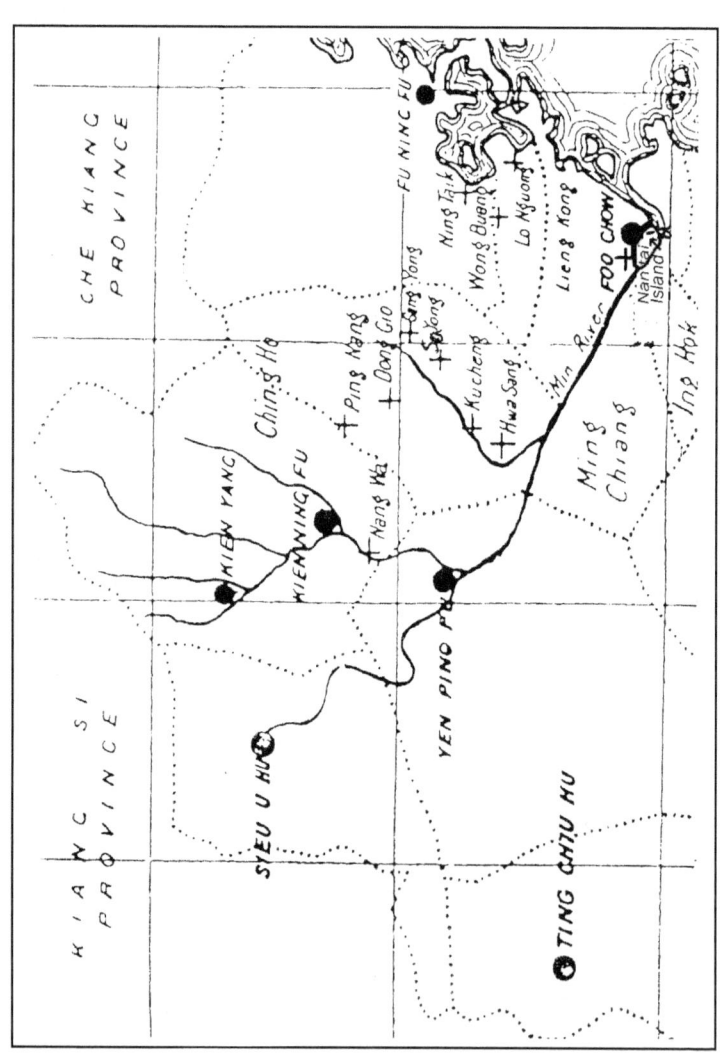

 China

By March 1886 Inie and Hessie were awaiting their appointment to their mission post. It was understood that they were to help Rev. Robert Stewart in Foochow since it was to his appeal for help that they owed their vocation.

Some time in the autumn they boarded ship for the first of many voyages to and from the Far East. They would spend from eight to twelve weeks on board and it was a far cry from modern-day cruises. The advent of refrigeration brought some variety to the menu and they would have booked cabins. But it is as well to recall the conditions in which poor Irish emigrants travelled to Australia at that time of the Potato Famine. One old steamer carried a thousand emigrants 'packed like herrings in a barrel', women in the stern and men and married couples in the bows, huddled together against the cold, sitting on rows of benches on deck all day.

Having sailed in September, our two missionaries arrived safely and came ashore at Foochow. The mission had been started in 1884 and besides the CMS there was also an American Mission. Foochow is situated at the mouth of the river Min,

Foochow Bridge

the main waterway of Fuhkien (Fujian) province. The walled

city is on the mainland but connected by the 'Bridge of Ten Thousand Ages'[16] to the island of Nan Tai, which is large enough to house a hundred Chinese villages packed together and also the foreign settlement.

Inie and Hessie were welcomed by Rev. and Mrs. Stewart[17] and introduced to the other missionaries. Then they settled down to learning Chinese. Mrs. Stewart was carrying on the Women's school started by Archdeacon Wolfe's wife and the new arrivals were to replace Miss Gough as her assistants. The ultimate aim of the school was to train Chinese women to be catechists or Bible Women who would return to their villages to spread the Good News. Chitnio, a young Chinese girl from Singapore was the Matron and she will appear again later in the story. She and Miss Gough had succeeded in entering many of the villages on the island. But the upper-class homes in the city were closed to them until the CEZ ladies had time to learn all the dos and don'ts of the strict Chinese etiquette. A Christian lady of the nobility, Mrs. Ahok, was able to instruct them in the niceties of social intercourse and introduce them to her friends and relatives in the city.

In some of the mansions they met five or six wives of a wealthy man, living in comparative harmony but each in her own apartments with her own children and servants. They were very curious to hear about English manners and customs; many had never seen a European. They never ventured out of doors except in sedan chairs, for all girls and women had their feet bound from an early age

Lady missionaries ready for the chair-ride

with the toes turned under to keep them small. They could only hobble along; this will explain why Inie with her easy stride was twice mistaken for a man.

The following April 1887 the sisters moved into a house which had been made ready for them and was to be the CEZMS headquarters in Foochow. Here all future probationers lived while they were learning the language and it was their home when, from time to time, persecution forced them to leave the up-country stations. The house was christened 'The Olives' and dedicated to God's service with a prayer meeting to which all the missionaries English and American were invited.

Inie herself comments on these early days in a letter written in 1917[18]:

When my sister and I arrived, we found Miss Bushel of the Female Education Society in charge of the Girls' School in the old telegraph house and Archdeacon Wolfe's daughter keeping house for her father and helping with the city work. These two were the only single ladies in our English mission. During our first summer there was a severe case of sunstroke in the American mission and there was not one trained nurse in the three missions available for the case.

One of the earliest events I recall of historical importance for the women's work in Fuhkien was the visit of the secretary of the CMS from Salisbury Square (Mr. Wright, I believe, was his name). A meeting was held in Archdeacon (then plain Mr.) Wolfe's house presided over by the CMS visitor and to it were invited all the missionaries of the American church in the settlement. The subject discussed was the possibility of extending the work for women throughout the country districts.

At first only gentlemen took part and there seemed to be among them great nervousness at the idea of ladies travelling about the country freely. It was gathered that in the English mission up till then only missionaries' wives travelling with their husbands had ever visited the country stations.

A question from the chair brought out the fact that there were American single ladies present who had done some itinerating work, and they were asked to give, from their experience, their opinion as to the possibility, desirability and utility of such work. After hearing what they had to say it was made quite clear that the work needed to be done, and while only women could do it, they certainly could!!

The meeting has often come back to me in the light of the Hwa Sang massacre (when Hessie and the Stewart family were martyred in 1895). I feel the danger was not ignored, but that, while the possible cost was counted, it was deliberately conceded that the work ought to be done. Rev. and Mrs. Stewart were present and full of enthusiasm for the promise it contained of a fuller development of the women's work.

A short while after the meeting Mr. Stewart arranged that my sister and I should accompany his wife on a visit to Kutien (Gutian) city while he remained at his post at the divinity school in Foochow. We hired a houseboat to Cui Cau and left early Monday morning hoping to reach Kutien by Thursday or Friday evening.[19] The river was flooded, there was no wind and a strong contrary current so progress was slow. On Thursday evening we were still far from halfway. We were almost despairing of getting on that week. But, thank God, by Friday midday we heard the wind rising and in a short while with sails set we were running before the wind and reached our anchorage by four--thirty in the afternoon in plenty of time to make all preparations for an early start Saturday morning so as to reach Kutien the same night.

I remember Mrs. Stewart taking our experience as a parable of the Christian life: when trusting in our own efforts we struggle and strive to overcome and make such miserable progress. But when we learn to open our heart to the Divine breath, how the impossible becomes at once so gloriously possible.

There was another thirty miles journey northward by sedan chair up a tributary of the Min. The narrow footpath wound along mountainsides, hung over ravines or skirted rivers. In wet weather it was so slippery that even the pigs had to be shod with straw sandals!!

Over the mountains…

Our travellers found the Mission house on one side of the river and the walled city on the other. They were welcomed by Mr. and Mrs. Bannister who were the first missionaries to reside there. The work was well advanced with a church in the city and several chapels in the surrounding villages. Mrs. Bannister had, from the start, opened her house to any woman who wished to visit and as many as fifty came in one morning. She had started a Women's School next to the church and a Girls' School, mainly for the daughters of Christians, though some non-Christians were received.

Inie saw the need for women missionaries. At the Sunday service there were very few women. In her report to the London office she wrote: 'At present ninety per cent of our Christians are men. The fact speaks for itself. It has been clearly proved that the women of China can only be reached by women. We ought to face this question and answer it before God.'

During the visit Mrs. Stewart took Inie with her to visit the village of Cui Kau.. The path led over the hills but they were unable to see much of the scenery because torrential rain made it necessary for them to be completely covered up in their sedan chairs. The coolies all but lost their footing on the slippery climb. After thirty miles they arrived and were welcomed into the houses of the Christians and found an opportunity to tell the Good News to the pagans as well As they visited several houses in one morning Inie found the hospitality alarming: so many cups of tea and trays of cakes and they will not take a refusal. Fortunately it was not a breach of etiquette to pocket what you could not eat; "and we had a good laugh afterwards as we turned out the spoils of the days visiting."

Soon after this in 1888 they passed their language tests and Inie and her sister were appointed to Kutien as their first mission post Their language studies never ceased, for no less than five dialects were spoken in that county .

Before leaving Foochow Hessie made a long expedition of which she has left an account, with a fellow-Dubliner, Clara Bradshaw, They went by launch northwards up the coast from Foochow and visited many of the villages inland. Hessie found her concertina a valuable aid attracting the crowds

Rev. Stewart had found a way of writing the sounds in Roman letters which helped the illiterate Chinese women as well as the missionaries. One of them, Miss Bryer, translated the New Testament into the Romanized Colloquial of Kien Ning in 1897 as well as a dictionary. Benjamina corrected the proofs during her furlough that year so that the Bible Society could print it.

Meanwhile Maude had finished her course at The Willows and was preparing to sail for China. She was to go to Shanghai to begin her language studies and help set up the work with women in the great cosmopolitan port. An anonymous donation had been given to the CEZ for that purpose. But for this gift funds were too short to expand the work in Chekiang province. So it was that when Benjamina applied for training she was allowed to go straight to Shanghai with Maude. The Newcombe sisters had already proved their worth - resourceful, well trained, eager to spread the Gospel and self-supporting.

On arrival they were given a Chinese house near the West gate and began to learn the language of South China. English was widely spoken in the great seaport with its wide spectrum of religions and moral standards. It was possible to be a missionary in China without learning the language and many chose that soft option, including Catholic bishops. But the result was disastrous because Christianity remained a foreign religion linked to so many humiliations imposed on China by European greed. The end result was the Boxer massacres of 1900.

In 1890 there was a question of sending Maude and Benso, as she was known in Chinese, to Ning Po, another of the Treaty Ports south of Shanghai. But the work there never got started and to their great joy they were sent south to join their sisters in Fukien. Maude joined Inie and Hessie in Kutien where they were in charge of the schools. It was a relief to have a trained nurse as any case of illness in the schools could be taken by the pagans as a sign that the local devils were angry.

In her 1889 report Inie wrote of the Women's School at Kutien:

There have been decided tokens of God's Spirit's work. When we contrast the women in the head class with what they were eighteen months ago, when they first joined the school, we are compelled to praise God for the wondrous change grace has wrought. They are now earnest, bright Christian women with an intelligent grasp of the truths of Christianity.

Of the six who left at the end of the course, three took on some kind of Christian work in their villages and three went to the Foochow mission for further training. During the whole year there was a severe influenza epidemic in the school and Maude was devotedly nursing the sick. One who was very ill and hardly likely to recover said to Inie: 'Missionary Lady, don't be sad about me; my body has no peace, but my heart is full of peace, for Jesus is there to comfort me.'

Besides their work in the schools Inie and Hessie went itinerating together, sharing the joy of telling the 'old, old story' to crowds of women. Hessie commented on their reactions: 'Never did the Lord's sufferings seem so real to myself as when I saw how they felt it. One woman shuddered all over when it came to the crown of thorns, the spitting and the scourging, and she said over and over again, "and He suffered it all willingly for us! Truly we must love Him and try to please Him" … An intense longing and passion for souls which I had heard others speak of, but never experienced myself, seemed to take possession of me.'

Rev.Stewart often said of Inie and her sisters, 'You could not find more devoted and successful missionaries anywhere', and of Hessie: 'From personal acquaintance with dear Hessie, I can say, she lived the Christ-life. He lived in her, He filled her being, He looked through her eyes, He spoke in and through her.' Someone else said of her after her death, 'Only to look at her photograph and one sensed the power and sweetness which emanated from her. She lived in the light of the Master's face and drew us into it'.

One subject of prayer and concern for the missionaries was the number of unwanted baby girls who were drowned, even though infanticide was illegal. Inie was horrified when she heard an old woman in a village counting up the number of babies she had killed. She wrote home early in 1889:

We have already rescued six little waifs. If there were someone who could give more time to this work, numbers might be saved yearly and trained in our loving Saviour's service. I began with two or three who were brought to me as soon as my intention became known. I shall be thankful if I can arouse the prayerful interest (of my readers) in these poor neglected and uncared-for little girl-babies. In Kutien alone between 700 and 800 babies under one month old are left yearly at the asylum opened by the government for the prevention of infanticide. Babies left there in cold, dirty cells are nursed by desperately poor women for a dollar a month and many die. In addition to these, who knows how many more baby girls are murdered at birth?

Babies left at the asylum are sold to poor families to provide a future wife for their son, and in order to support the baby-wife, they frequently give up their own girl-baby to the same fate.

Our party now consists of ten little girls. Of these, one is already safe in the arms of Jesus. Another, we fear, will be difficult to rear. It was found on a hill-top just as the father was about to throw it into a hole. By the time it was brought to us it seemed nearly half-dead.

In 1891 Inie wrote again:

It is with difficulty we keep our number of little foundlings from increasing more rapidly. It is becoming very necessary to have some settled home for these little waifs. The last nine months I have had four of them living with me in my native house in Kutien. The other six are out in the city and neighbourhood in the charge of different women.

Room for the tinies was made in a small house and towards the end of 1891 Miss Nisbet became 'mother' to the wee waifs. Hessie wrote of them:

It is a pretty picture, five little, tiny tots gathered round Miss Nisbet singing 'Jesus loves me'. Then they climb on her knee, lean their heads on her shoulder, and repeat their evening prayer.

By this time there were thirteen of these rescued girls and a house was built on a hilltop to accommodate forty, believing that God would provide for His lambs. Hessie christened the house 'The Birds' Nest'.

In a letter to Mina, from Sang Yong, Benjamina told how the missionaries found a tiny baby on their doorstep and suspected a very poor Christian couple in the village. But the father maintained that their baby had died and he had buried it. The Chinese pastor insisted on seeing the grave and unearthed a lump of clay wrapped in cloth. The poor man fell at his feet sobbing with shame, but his pastor only said, 'I still love you'. Next Sunday a collection was taken up to help rear the baby.

8 Kien Ning

One or two new recruits were by 1889 joining the mission[20] so it became possible for Inie to visit the Kien Ning prefecture over the mountains to the north--west. The way led through a pass 3,000 feet up and descended into the broad valley of another tributary of the Min terraced with rice-fields. The great Fu city of Kien Ning (modern spelling Jian Ow) was fiercely anti-Christian. No missionary had lived there since 1875 when Pastor Ling and his helpers had been cruelly beaten and expelled. But in the five walled towns and the numerous villages which surrounded it, it had been possible for CMS missionaries to set up mission posts and a hospital at Nang Wa. Inie's visit only high—lighted the need for more women missionaries.

On her return it was decided that Benso should move to Cieng Bau, one of the villages near Kien Ning city and Inie would follow as soon as she could be replaced . Benso then moved to Nang Wa.

An incident which Inie relates seems to prove that she very soon began to wear Chinese dress – wide trousers and long tunic – which was more or less the same for men and women. Before moving to Kien Ning Prefecture late 1889, Inie and her fellow-Dubliner, Miss Bradshaw, visited Lo Yuan, chief town of a county due east of Kutien, which lies in a deep valley one end of which is open to the sea. It had been evangelised by the CMS in the 1870s, but persecution had left only the most fervent Christians. But ten years later our two CEZ missionaries were met by friendly, curious crowds in the villages they visited. In the town of Lo Yuan however, Inie noticed that the men in the streets were particularly unpleasant when she walked through the town accompanied by Mrs. Chitnio Ling, the young wife of the Chinese pastor of Kutien.

I had several times noticed the men in the streets were very rude and this special afternoon on our way home we had to pass a group who were specially unpleasant-looking. They called at us in passing. Little Ling Sengli, who usually took no notice, suddenly turned and poured forth her wrath in a perfect torrent of Chinese that I could only half follow. Then seizing my arm she hurried on home, rushed upstairs, burst into tears and wept unrestrainedly for long before we could fully grasp what had happened. When somewhat quietened she explained that the men, taking me for a man, had called her by a vile name for walking out in the street with me. Until we had met Sengli, my companion had always been an old woman.

After a while she brightened up and said how for long she had wished to go out into the city and work for God but her husband had refused on the grounds that she was too young. Now she had the chance she must not mind the insults. We were able to send her an old Christian woman as companion so that she could continue the work she had begun with us.[21]

Chitnio (Sengli) was a girl from the school in Singapore. Her husband died from the effects of the beating he received in Kien Ning city. They had only been married two years.

At the end of 1889 when Inie and Frances Johnson took up residence at Ciong Bau[22], sixteen miles from Kien Ning city, their first task was to learn the local dialect. Fortunately they found three girls who had just returned from the Foochow school and could speak both dialects and so act as interpreters for the first few weeks. Curious women came in crowds, friends were soon made, especially as Frances was a nurse and could help the sick. Soon they were able to start a class for the women and later baptisms followed.

Inie had for language teacher a young Christian man from

the city, whose father became very interested. He came to Ciong Bau to beg the missionaries to visit his house and teach the women of his household. No missionary had entered the city since the persecutions of 1875, but our two ladies braved the dangers and set out in closely-curtained sedan chairs and passed unnoticed through the gates of the forbidden city.

They were courteously received in a refined but unostentatious home: 'blue gowns, not silks'. Sumptuous repasts were served on old china on a polished blackwood table. They ate with ivory chopsticks while the host stood by apologising for the meanness of the elegant meal: 'Not fit for you to eat, the remains of yesterday's very coarse fare'!

Then they met the women relatives in an inner room and shared with them the Good News of the Christian message. The evening ended with prayer - prayer *for* Kien Ning had never ceased, but this was prayer *in* Kien Ning.

In 1886 Dr. Rigg had opened a hospital at Nang Wa fifteen miles south of the city where Benjamina was stationed for several years. In 1890 he opened another hospital staffed by Chinese only a few minutes from the city gates where public prayer and preaching were carried on every day.

There were fifteen villages within a three-mile radius of the city and Inie and Frances visited them all. At first the women came to listen to them. But often their husbands forbade contact with the foreign 'devils' and beat them if they persisted. Inie recounts an incident on one such visit which must have been frightening: They were staying in a house outside the village and had gone to bed when they were awakened by the noise of men shouting. As the sound grew nearer they heard shouts of 'Foreign Devils – Kill!' and they hurriedly dressed and prepared for the worst. But after the crowd had surrounded the house shouting ferociously, the noise suddenly stopped and the men went away quietly. Next morning Inie and her companion went into the village and asked a Christian what it was all about. Apparently there was a sick boy who seemed to be dying and the villagers thought the local devil must be angry with the 'foreign devils'. To placate him they decided to pretend to kill his rivals!

In the Spring of 1891 Inie and Frances Johnson visited Ching Ho, a large city fifty miles north-east of Kien Ning city, hoping it would be a better centre for their work. They were met by crowds curious to hear about the Christian religion. Apart from the hospital there were no mission centres in the area. Inie wrote[23] in her annual report of August 1891:

Here in Kien Ning Prefecture, no church is established with its attendant schools and classes. Can we plant some of these things? The whole district is more or less opposed to Christianity. Renting a house is always a matter of difficulty but possession is often still more troublesome. It has however been proved in cases like these that ladies will be quietly tolerated where men and even native helpers from another district will be promptly expelled. Is there not in this view of the case a call for *our* Society to go forward?

In the autumn they managed to rent a house in Ching Ho[24], but it was not ready to be occupied until the following Easter. Their tenancy was very short, for on the fourth day trouble began. A crowd of men and boys pushed their way into the house demanding that the two missionaries leave. They refused and held out for three days. Then the Mandarin intervened and carried them off to the safety of his yamen (women's quarters). Two days later they were recalled to Nang Wa. After their departure the mob wrecked the house. The disturbance in Ching Ho was followed by a more serious riot in Kien Ning in which Dr. Rigg nearly lost his life. It seemed wiser to withdraw mission-aries from the whole district.

Frances Johnson joined Benjamina[25] at Nang Wa where Miss Bryer was working on a translation of the New Testament. Inie, who was due for furlough the following year, returned over the mountains to Kutien. It may have been on this journey that the following incident occurred which made a lasting impression on her. She tells the story in the account of her conversion written at the age of seventy:

One day while on a long day's chair ride, we stopped for rest and lunch near the top of a steep mountain pass over which the road led. I left the chair and the coolies having a more prolonged rest and smoke and proceeded alone up the side of the mountain. I was shortly joined by a Chinese Christian lad. One has to live in a pagan land to realise to the full the joy of unexpected Christian companionship. I soon discovered he was a Catholic, born of Christian parents, and a thoroughly well instructed Christian rejoicing in his faith. On enquiring as to his teacher, I was given a word-picture of a Catholic priest, a European, who had given himself wholly to the people during a long life of loving service. When my coolies caught up with me as we reached the top of the pass, I had to part from the lad, but I carried away two pictures in my mind: that of the old priest and his devoted, enthusiastic pupil. This was my first conversation with a Catholic on the subject of religion; my part was listening; his, all unconsciously, was revealing.

New horizons

On arrival at Kutien Inie received a great welcome - she was, after all, the senior of the band of CEZ missionaries in Fukien. She had to give all the news of Kien Ning and the work achieved in face of great opposition. But she was cheered by the news of a steady flow of new recruits coming from Britain: Miss Bryer, Miss Rodd and Miss Fleming for Nang Wa. At Kutien, Miss Nisbet was in charge of the home for foundlings called 'The Birds Nest'. Miss Codrington and Miss Tolley were learning Chinese, as were Miss Marshall and Miss Stewart. They had answered the appeal of a brave Chinese lady of the upper class, Mrs. Ahok of Foochow[26], who had agreed to accompany Miss Bradshaw, one of the first Dublin recruits who was going home on sick leave. She said: 'I thought to myself – the people in England who have so much light themselves, surely do not know that so many people in China are living in the dark, are dying without God. If I go and tell them myself perhaps they will believe me.' She spoke at one hundred meetings in three months, Mrs. Stewart acting as her interpreter, and the appeal they both made touched many hearts. In the next four years no less than sixteen new recruits went to Fukien.

Soon after Inie got back to Kutien, Rev. Stewart called a meeting of all the missionaries and Chinese church workers from the districts of Kutien and Ping Nang to discuss needs and how to meet them[27].

A mixed assembly they were that cold winter's day: the city folk in their silks and furs, the Bible Women neat and simple and the country delegates with many coats, winter hoods buttoned under their chin, clutching fire-baskets and raising many a ripple of laughter with their stories. But they knew how to plead their cause – the women's cause. 'Send us teachers to help our women so that our homes may be Christian homes'. They pleaded especially for Sang Iong (Shan Yang) and the whole district over the mountains to the east of Kutien known as the East Road.

The following month Inie was sent to visit the East Road and took with her Miss Codrington and Miss Burroughs so that she could help them learn the local dialect. They were approaching the town of Sang Iong carried in sedan chairs and had reached the gates when a violent thunder-storm broke over them. Inie relates:

> My terrified coolies rushed me into the first open door that they saw and fled, leaving me for the first time in my experience alone in a heathen home with no Chinese Christian as guide and companion. The master of the house entreated me to leave the chair and enter his hall and I acceded. On supplying me with a seat, he proceeded to sit down near me, to my discomfiture, as I knew this was not 'en regle'. He leaned over enquiring confidentially, 'Sir, how old are you?' The question I did not mind, being the most usual start to making friends. But the 'Sir' enlightened me that I was supposed to be a man. I was fairly frightened. I could not sustain the character and hastily informed my host that I was a foreign woman and would much like to see his wife. He understood at once and to my great relief, went to his wife's room and called her out. I followed and finding she would not venture out, I boldly entered and began trying to make her understand. By the time the rain was over and my coolies returned, we were quite friendly. A few minutes brought me to the Catechist's house where I found my companions already arrived and anxiously wondering what had become of me[28].

There was tremendous excitement in the town next day[29]. The missionaries were beset by the usual curious crowds anxious to get a glimpse of the foreigners. During their stay of two weeks the only accommodation was the attic of a Christian's house with rats for company; they were often blinded by the smoke from the kitchen below. But some good work was done and services held for the women. They prepared the ground for a permanent mission with church and schools where Maude and Miss Burroughs were to live for many years. Benjamina joined them in 1903 and both sisters are buried there.

Inie and her companions made a tour of the villages and it may be that one of them was the scene of the surprising conversion that she related in her old age[30]. It seems that in one of the villages they had set up a little chapel and a few people came to it. But all the time they were annoyed and persecuted by a very unfriendly pagan Headman and his friends As time went on and no progress was being made they almost decided to go elsewhere when a strange thing happened.

The next Sunday they were in their little chapel to give instruction to the few Chinese who usually came. They were about to begin when the door opened and to their amazement, in came the Headman leading a procession of all the notables and other villagers. Nothing was said as they took their places and they said nothing but were obviously friendly – a great change! After the service the smiling Headman was asked what had happened, and he told an extraordinary story. The evening before, he and his supporters had been 'wondering' about the missionaries, why they had come and so on – when there was a knock at the door. On opening it they saw a man they had never seen before. He was very dignified, appeared to be a man of great authority and, strangest of all, spoke beautiful Mandarin. He told them they must go to the mission chapel where they would be told the truth and what they must believe – so they had come! The man told them nothing about himself or where he had come from; he simply said what he had to say and turned to go. They asked his name and he simply said 'Paul' and nothing more.

From then on they had no more trouble, conversions began to happen and all went well with the Headman as a willing helper. Inie recounted that some of the missionaries' reactions, besides praising God, were less noble: 'Fancy St. Paul' they said, 'coming down from heaven to convert that old villain who has given us so much trouble and not coming to see us!' They knew what the elder brother of the Prodigal Son felt like!

During these months of the winter of 1892-1893 there also occurred an encounter which was to change Inie's life. She tells the story in the account of her conversion to Catholicism.

Some time later I once again came into contact with Catholic missionary activity. It was in a distant part of the province where a different dialect was spoken. I was helping two newly arrived fellow-workers to start learning the language of the district which had been chosen as their field of work. After three months steady work at the language, we planned and carried out a tour of the district visiting a number of out-lying stations where there were small groups of Christians belonging to our mission. We had reached our most distant station and finding it had never been visited by any European missionary, decided to stay for a few days.

One afternoon we were surprised by the visit of a Spanish Catholic priest accompanied by his Chinese curate. He explained that, having heard of our arrival, he had walked over to see us, hoping that he might be able to use his mother tongue and hear it spoken again. Alas, we did not know Spanish and we were obliged to keep to Chinese as a means of conversation. We got afternoon tea and had a long talk in which we were the interested listeners. Encouraged by our evident desire for information, he told us of the gradual growth of the work since the time, six years before, when he was appointed curate to a Chinese priest shortly after his arrival at the port. He told us how he had lived with this priest who had taught him the language, and that, just a year before, the Bishop had divided the huge district into two parishes, and that since then, he and his Chinese curate had been working away at their half. As we sat listening, he seemed to me to be an embodiment of heroic self-denial, and we watched him go with feelings of heart-felt veneration.

Early in 1893, having returned to Kutien, Inie said good--bye to Rev. Stewart and his family and all the friends she had made there, little guessing that it would be for an absence of eighteen years. She and Hessie embarked at Foochow and spent several weeks on the voyage home. While it was a welcome rest after seven years of hard work, life on board seemed so luxurious after the lack of basic comforts they had accepted in God's service and the dire poverty of the people of rural China.

They met people on the ship who could empathize with their enthusiasm for spreading the Gospel, but so many others whose minds were closed and cluttered with worldly ambitions. In view of Inie's surprising decisions this year one has to remember that coming back to Western materialism from working in the Third World is as much of a culture shock as going. But at first our two returning missionaries had their minds and hearts full of the joy of seeing dear Aunt Lily, Mina and Lucy again. All the family were there to meet them off the ferry from Holyhead.

But one of their loved ones was not there and there were tears as they heard again all the details of their brother Charlie's accident and death[31]. So young – he had only graduated a year before and gained his M.A. He had been holidaying on Howth Island across Dublin Bay and had fallen from rocks. He was taken by boat to Kingstown where he had lingered only a few days. They had all been with him at the end. If Aunt Lily had a favourite it was Charlie but she took her grief to the Lord in silent prayer and set about giving the weary travellers a warm welcome in the old home, with the prospect of six months of real rest and relaxation.

In the days that followed there was much catching up on news and stories of the missions to be told – omitting, of course, the more worrying details of their adventures. Then there were meetings with the support group, the Hibernian Auxiliary of the CEZMS, to appeal for funds and particularly for building schools in the new missions of Sang Iong and Sa long.

So, one has to ask, what went wrong? Why did Inie during this first furlough decide to abandon ship and resign from the CEZMS and the missionary life in China that she so loved? Why especially when it meant parting from her three sisters?

She herself gives her reasons, but the question still arises: why did Divine Providence bring her, through a chance encounter, to such a painful decision? This is how she explains:

> I started soon on my way home. And in the excitement of the journey and the homecoming I thought no more of my meeting the priest. But a seed had been sown and soon it began to manifest its presence. Every time a careless sneer, an unkind criticism or a harsh judgment against the Catholic Church, its faith or its priesthood, was uttered in my hearing, it roused in me at once a feeling of opposition. And how often these remarks occur in the conversation of most religious Protestants[32] I think they hardly realise themselves. I began to realise that Protestantism consists primarily in opposing Roman Catholicism and I renounced it as a false religion from that time. But, though no longer a Protestant, the idea never entered my head to become a Catholic myself. And, as far as I can judge, had my health held out enabling me to throw myself into my missionary work as vigorously as before, I would never have got beyond the 'negative position'.[33]

With her radical, honest, no-compromise character, Inie knew she had cut loose from her former prejudices, and as these were so much a part of the Church in which she had been brought up, she could no longer in conscience be an accredited emissary of the Evangelical Church of Ireland. If only one could just be a Christian, to preach Christ, lead people to Him and what C.S.Lewis called 'Mere Christianity'.

What she had heard of the Salvation Army filled her with hope[34]. She gives no details of her first meeting with them beyond that she heard with interest of their work in India. But from the fact that she had already joined their ranks on December 5th the same year as she returned from China, one might be right in guessing that she heard of them on the very voyage home. Some fellow traveller, glad of Christian conversation, may have passed on to her his enthusiasm for the new movement.

William Booth had never set out to found a new sect or denomination, but only to draw people to Christ and salvation. Many as a result of his preaching returned to the church of their childhood, but many more stayed with the Army and joined its ranks. Many of his converts were too poor and ragged to be acceptable in churches. The 'Articles of War' which prospective recruits were expected to sign contain all the basic beliefs common to all Churches professing the divinity of Christ. In 1882 Major Frederick Tucker took a party of Salvationists to India, and from the first centre in Bombay, in three years had come sixteen others, with the 'War cry' translated into four of the Indian languages.

And so the die was cast. Inie formally resigned from the CEZMS. It must have been a heartrending decision for her and her sisters especially for Hessie who would have to return to China without her. Yet they knew that Inie could not go against her conscience and had to follow the Lord wherever He was leading her. They themselves had no problem: God had put them where they were and there He sanctified them and made them fruitful for His kingdom. All three died in China, faithful to the end.

 # Ꞩessie

1893 passed all too quickly. Somehow Inie broke the news to her family and friends that she would not be returning to China the following Spring. Then she left for London and on December 5th began a new chapter of her life.

In May 1894 Hessie also left for London. The parting was lightened by the thought that Maude and Benjamina would soon be due for furlough. Hessie had to address a meeting on May 5th in St. James's Hall. Then she boarded ship[35], crossing to Canada where she met William and then sailed to China from Vancouver. Probably Inie had already been sent to India.

On arrival in Kutien she took up again the supervision of the Girls' Boarding School, the first of its kind, which she herself had founded in 1889. It was a small, low, lath-and-plaster building for thirty-five girls on the lovely wooded hill, the Hill of Righteousness where the CMS and CEZ compound was built across the river from the city. On the mountain 2,000 feet above Kutien Rev. Stewart had bought a piece of land and some cottages to be a holiday rest-home for the missionaries in the hot season.[36] The village was called Hwa Sang, Flowery Hill, but it became the Hill of Glory. Rev. Bannister had a large bungalow and a smaller one built beyond the village.

During Hessie's absence in 1893, Maude and the two ladies who had been with Inie when they met the Dominican priest, spent three months at Sa Iong (Siyang), thirty miles from Kutien in the East Road district.[37] A big rambling house was rented at a nominal sum because it was said to be haunted! Crowds came daily to see the foreign women and all heard the Gospel message. Maude opened a dispensary which opened up hearts and homes. Besides the usual ailments she often had to treat cases of opium poisoning and saved many lives. About opium addiction Hessie wrote home:

Hwa Sang Missionaries' Sanatorium

House on left occupied by CEZ Missionaries; house on right, by Rev and Mrs Stewart

I much doubt if there is any place where opium has not penetrated.[38] I can only speak from experience of this province. One of my own teachers compared its ravages to the last plague of Egypt; as she said, there is scarcely a family without a victim to this awful scourge. When she questioned me with horror as to the report that this poison came from England, I did not dare to tell her the whole truth: that our Christian government obtained a portion of its revenue from the sale. I only said that there were men in England and elsewhere who love money more than God, but that truly Christian people were very sorry for the Chinese.

In 1839 the Imperial Government had declared war on England for allowing the opium trade to use her ports. But by 1844 the Chinese were forced to open five of her ports to foreigners, including Foochow, and the opium trade continued.

Besides a Sunday School, Miss Codrington pioneered at Sa Yong the idea of a short-term residential school for women. Some extra lath-and-plaster rooms were added to the Mission house. The women brought their babies with them and stayed about three months. This was the first of many Station Classes held in different parts of Fukien.

At the end of 1893 Maude was replaced by Miss Tolley and moved ten miles further east to Sang Iong where she was joined by Miss Burroughs[39]. They were the first resident missionaries there and it was probably there that Inie and Miss Burroughs and Miss Codrington had met the Spanish priest the previous winter.

Rev. Stewart said they could only stay one year but such crowds came, drawn to the services out of curiosity and then stayed, that he said, 'God has opened a wide door for you here and I cannot remove you'. They stayed fifteen years and both Maude and Benjamina died there. When Maude was due for her first furlough in 1895 the people petitioned to keep her and she did not go home until 1902. It was at Sang Iong that she adopted a little Chinese baby, a little girl she christened Grace.

In the 1890s war between China and Japan was going on and the Japanese were approaching Foochow in 1895.[40] This gave courage to various rebel groups to engage in terrorist attacks against their own imperial government which was hated by the people. Among these secret societies was one named 'The Vegetarians', known to be recruiting in large numbers at this time.

Rev. and Mrs Stewart had been on furlough from 1891 and arrived back from a lecture tour in Canada in 1893. Soon after this their four youngest children arrived from Dublin in the care of their nurse, Lena Yellop, an orphan brought up in the Home run by Mrs Smyly, mother of Mrs Stewart. Another baby, Hilda Sylvia, was born to the Stewarts in September 1894. They loved Kutien and said that in the whole world, God could not have chosen for them a more healthful and beautiful spot.

But the storms were gathering, and in a letter dated April 8th 1895, Rev. Stewart wrote:[41]

> We have been having some rather exciting times here lately. Ten days ago I was called up at 4 o' clock in the morning by our native clergyman and other Christians, who had crossed the river to our house to bring the startling news that the Vegetarian rebels were expected at daybreak to storm Kutien, and that the gateways of the city were being blocked with timber and stone as fast as possible.
>
> At the time the alarm was given, we had, with women, girls and children, nearly one hundred sleeping in our compound. The rebels were expected in an hour! What was to be done?
>
> As we talked and prayed and planned, the dawn began to break; then came the rain in torrents. Remembering the fear the Chinese have of getting wet, we said to one another, 'That rain will be our protection'.

At daybreak we roused the schools, and after a hasty meal, all left in a sad procession to cross the river in a small boat, which came backwards and forwards for them, until at last the whole party had reached the other side. It was a long business all in the rain, and then the wall had to be climbed by a ladder, for by this time the blocking of the gateways was complete. Only one part of the broken-down wall had not been built up to its full height and the only ladder available would otherwise have been too short by several feet and we could never have got the women with their cramped feet and the children over the wall.

For the next three days the wall was guarded by bands of citizens, armed with the best weapons they could find: rusty swords and three-pronged forks. Those days were anxious ones. Then the gates were opened, but no one believes we have seen the end of the matter – probably it is only the beginning.

The British and American Consuls advised all the women missionaries to go back to Foochow. This they did reluctantly and travelled down to Cui Kau on the river Min, but while waiting for a boat to take them down to Foochow they received a message from Rev. Stewart to return as the danger was over.

By May life in the Mission compound at Kutien was resumed and the schools were functioning normally. Rev. Stewart arranged that the usual holiday in the great heat of July should be taken at the cottages near the mountain village of Hwa Sang, 2,000 feet above Kutien. The children were sent on ahead with their nurse; Hessie joined them when she returned from three weeks itinerating and Robert and Louisa Stewart closed the mission and walked the eight miles in the cool of the evening arriving at midnight.

Sharing the larger bungalow were the Stewarts and their children baby Hilda, Evan four, Herbert nearly six, Millicent ten and Kathleen twelve. Also the nurse Lena and the two Saunders sisters, Nellie and Topsy, who belonged to an

Australian missionary society. In the other cottage were the five CEZ missionaries, Hessie, Flora Codrington, Elsie Marshall, Annie Gordon and Lucy Stewart. All except Hessie had only been in China a few years and were probably in their early twenties; Hessie was thirty-three.

Unknown to them in their peaceful retreat, the rebels had attacked a village and the mandarin appealed for protection.

Two hundred soldiers arrived in Kutien on July 25th. The rebels defiantly fortified a nearby hill-top with their flags visible from the city. A necromancer called Long Nails was urging the leaders to attack the Christians. Lots were drawn and Hwa. Sang was drawn on three successive nights.

The future martyrs knew nothing of this but they were prepared.

During the first week of their holiday, besides resting, they arranged a series of spiritual colloquies coinciding with the programme of the Keswick Convention which was taking place that week in England. Joining in their prayerful discussions was another CMS missionary, Rev. H. Phillips, who was staying in the village, and Miss Hartford, an American missionary who had a house nearby. The theme of the last day of July was the Transfiguration of the Lord Jesus on Mount Tabor, and at the close of the Communion Service they all renewed their dedication with the prayer: 'Here we offer and present unto Thee, Lord, ourselves, our souls and bodies, to be a reasonable, holy and lively sacrifice unto Thee.'

Early next morning about 6 am the little girls were out gathering flowers for Herbert's sixth birthday to be celebrated with a picnic, when they heard men shouting and saw the crowd of rebels coming up the hill armed with spears. Millicent ran to give the alarm but Kathleen was caught and dragged by her hair. She struggled free and ran into their room with Millie and bolted the door. They heard the men break into the house and kill their parents, and then Lena and Nellie Saunders.

Kathleen was hiding under the bed and escaped

unharmed, but Millie was beaten and stabbed in the knee-joint. The men were looting in all the rooms and found some Kerosene which they sprinkled everywhere and then left to surround the other cottage. Kathleen and Millicent went past the bodies of their parents and bravely pulled the baby from under the nurse's body and carried her out of the house. They got little Evan who was only slightly hurt, and badly-injured Herbert, out of the house before it went up into flames.

Annie Gordon, who had been reading outside, gave the alarm in the other cottage. They managed to bolt the doors but there were eighty men watching them through the windows. Topsy Saunders had joined them and they helped each other to get dressed. Then they all knelt in prayer, led by Hessie.

When the men broke into the house and began looting, the five women got out of the back door and were surrounded by men with spears. At first they asked for money, but the leader ordered them to kill. Flora Codrington told the others not to be afraid. 'Sisters, never mind, we are all going Home together.' Then she acted on the advice she had given them and fell down at the first blow and pretended to be dead. All the others died and the house was set ablaze.

Hessie had tried to break through the men in her anxiety to get to Mrs Stewart and was stabbed to death and thrown down an embankment. When the signal was given, the assassins left with their loot, waving a banner they had made out of a sheet bearing Chinese characters: 'China's dragon goes to war with Christians' Jesus'.

Flora Codrington, badly wounded, had fainted, but when she regained consciousness and found all was quiet, she tried to drag the bodies of her Sisters away from the burning house. When her strength failed, she got to Miss Hartford's house with the help of a Chinese man. Kathleen carried the baby and the little boys there and got help for Millicent, who could not walk. There they were joined by Rev. Phillips who had come up from the village. He helped to bind up their wounds and went to cover the bodies to protect them from the sun. The whole tragic episode was over by 7.30 am and a messenger went down the mountain to Kutien for help with the wounded.

Dr.Gregory at Kutien got the news at 12.30 and could hardly believe it. He could not persuade any chair coolies to take him up to Hwa Sang for fear of the rebels. So at 2.30 he set out on foot alone.

Immediately a chair and escort of thirteen soldiers was organised. They only arrived at Hwa Sang at 7.30 p.m. and Dr.Gregory was aghast at the wounds of the victims and survivors, "hacked and stabbed beyond recognition" He and Rev.Phillips worked until midnight dressing wounds and obtainng coffins. At 1.30 a.m. they went up to the burnt-out cottages and performed the last sad duties for the martyred missionaries, placing the charred remains of Robert and Louisa together in one coffin. They worked until 8 a.m. and spent the rest of the day persuading enough bearers to undertake the 15 mile trek down to Cui Kau.

By 3 pm the following day, August 2nd, the doctor thought they had recovered sufficient strength to start down the mountain-side, carried on stretchers. They were weak from loss of blood – Flora Codrington was badly wounded in face, neck arm and thigh. Little Herbert was so badly wounded that he died on the journey. 'How glad Father and Mother will be to see him', said brave, suffering Millicent. Kathleen carried the baby most of the way.

From three in the afternoon they continued that terrible, steep descent for fifteen miles until it was too dark to go on. They rested at a Chinese inn for supper and a Chinese woman came to Flora and said to her, 'Sister, don't think all your work is spoiled; the women of Kutien are weeping, they are so touched. Now many will believe.' The girls in the boarding school were mourning the loss of Hessie and each of the dead was an incalculable loss to the Mission. When Millicent was told that one of the CEZ missionaries would accompany them back to Ireland, she protested that no one could be spared and that the stewardess would help them care for the little ones. Such was the heroism of those children that a Chinese man said of one of them, 'Truly, she has greatly received the Holy Spirit'.

After the fifteen miles down the mountainside, they rejoined the tributary of the Min below Kutien and another ten miles brought the sad procession to Cui Kan, where they waited for the boat sent up from Foochow. They arrived there on Sunday Aug 4th at midday and Rev. Bannister announced to the waiting crowd: 'Nearly all of them are in heaven', and read out the ten names.

The five survivors were taken at once to the hospital. Kathleen was exhausted, but the baby would not at first be parted from her. In spite of all the love with which she was surrounded, she went to join her mother a few days later. Mildred hovered between life and death, but in answer to much prayer and devoted care, she and Flora made a wonderful recovery. Flora returned to Fukien in less than four years and gave another Twenty five years of devoted service to the mission.

The funeral took place on August 6th in the cool of the early morning at the English cemetery. One long grave received the seven coffins with a low brick partition between each. Beautiful white wreaths covered them and the epitaph on Hessie's, composed by Rev. Phillips ran as follows:

Her leading characteristic had been spirituality of mind and her principal theme of conversation was the Lord's Return. The Master is come and calleth for thee'.

The four rebel leaders were brought to justice and before they died, a Chinese Christian visited each one in prison and spoke about the Good Thief. The children's aunt, who had come to take the children back to Dublin, sent them a message: 'Tell them from me, that we freely forgive them, for

Mrs. Louisa Stewart
Ireland

Hessie Newcombe
Ireland

Rev. Robert Stewart
Ireland

Flora Lucy Stewart
England

Mary Anne Christian Gordon
Australia

Elsie Marshall,
England

Harriet Eleanor Saunders
Australia

"BE THOU FAITHFUL UNTO
DEATH. AND I WILL GIVE
THEE A CROWN OF LIFE."

Elizabeth Maud Saunders
Australia

we know it was the devil in them who caused them to do it'. She said that the children frequently said the same and felt no resentment.

Miss Smyly and Miss Leslie took Flora and the children safely back to Britain, arriving on November 11th. Flora was to return to China for many more years and outlived all the Newcombe sisters. Around 1928 she wrote some notes on the family which preserved much information about their childhood. Although she noted that Inie became a Roman Catholic, she must have lost touch and presumed that she died while living with cousins at Rathgar.

The news of Hessie's death would have taken some time to reach the family and what must have been the grief of Aunt Lily and her sisters so soon after losing Charlie! Inie had just arrived in Tokyo when she received the sad but glorious news.

This tragedy, which robbed the mission of its leader, Rev. Robert Stewart, caused the immediate withdrawal of all the CEZ ladies from the up-country stations and the suspension of all the work except in Foochow for several months[42]. During this time they found plenty to do helping in the Foochow schools and hospitals. Miss Bryer spent her enforced leisure completing her translation of the New Testament into a Romanized version of the Kien Ning dialect. When Christmas passed and news came through that all was calm again, the Consul decided that some of the CEZ ladies could go back after the Chinese New Year, 1896. Maude and Benjamina were due for home-leave that year but Maude offered to go back to Kutien instead. Apart from the real need of her experience to get the work started again, her little adopted daughter was too young to travel and she was looking forward to taking her home to meet her new family.

So Benjamina set off alone and delivered Miss Bryer's translation to the British and Foreign Bible Society in London.

The proofs arrived before she was due to return so she delayed her return until February 1897 in order to correct them. Her meetings with the support group of Auxiliaries in Dublin had the consoling result that a collection was made to build a school in Sang Iong to be called The Hessie Newcombe Memorial School. A similar collection financed the building of a Boys' School in Kutien in memory of Robert Stewart.

When Benjamina returned to China she was appointed to Ciong Bau, a mission post in the Kien Ning district. It was here that she received a sad short letter from Aunt Lily to say that dear Lucy had gone to God. Poor Aunt had accepted those nine little children as a gift from God and her life's work and already He had taken back three of them.

There followed two years of peaceful upbuilding for the missions. In the Spring of 1899 Benjamina was called to Kutien to take over the itinerating of a district south-west of the city. This entailed visiting the villages where there were groups of Christians. There were twelve chapels and three day schools run by women who had been through the CEZ schools in the city. Mostly the journeys were made on foot and she often thought of how the Gospel was first preached in the villages of Galilee.

Not long after she left Ciong Bau the clouds began to gather for a storm[43], the fore-runner of a much more terrible storm, the Boxer uprising which claimed the lives of thousands of Christian martyrs. Those visiting the out-stations were the first to notice a change in the atmosphere: slander and persecution of Christians, rumours that the foreigners had killed a woman who had died in hospital, etc. After a long weary journey over rough mountain tracks they might find no hospitable lodging and have to sleep in the open. 'The Son of Man has nowhere to lay His head.' Miss Gardner was nearly killed by a madman who badly injured the Bible woman who defended her. The latent anti-foreigner feeling throughout the prefecture was being fanned into flame by the Secret Societies and was soon blazing. Dr. Rigg quickly made arrangements for the four CEZ ladies to leave: Misses Johnson, Darley, Gardner and Colston. The two at Ciong Bau, Miss Rodd and Miss Bryer hurriedly sent the girls home, closed the school and walked the twelve miles to Nang Wa in pouring rain. Dr. Rigg and Dr. Pakenham stayed behind, but all the CMS and CEZ missionaries arrived safely in Foochow. But the Chinese Christians suffered: some were stoned to death, the Mission house and church were burned down and the hospital looted.

After four months the storm had passed and the missionaries were allowed to return to Nang Wa and begin rebuilding. Their dedication and self-sacrifice were not lost on the notables of the city and they came to the conclusion that the foreigners were fated to enter their city and it was useless to keep them out. 'Heaven permits them to be here; it is useless for us to try to oppose them.' So forty of the head men of Kien Ning city met with the Mandarins and, in the presence of Dr. Rigg and Mr. Phillips signed a bond promising to protect and respect foreigners, native Christians and mission building, not only in the city itself, but in the whole district.

The mission was built up again and Miss Darley wrote in praise of the Chinese Christians who had stood firm during the persecution and held Sunday services openly in their villages. But the following year 1900 the missionaries were once again ordered to withdraw as the Boxers swept through northern China killing and destroying. Outraged by the humiliations imposed on China by the European powers, the Crown Prince persuaded the old Empress to unleash the Boxers and give orders to the army to support them. Thanks to the courage and compassion of the two northern Viceroys, the wire received by the Chinese authorities in the southern provinces did not read as intended: 'Exterminate the foreigners' but 'Protect the foreigners' – the change of one character! They both paid the penalty with their lives but saved how many?

The uprising was suppressed in August of the same year by ruthless, bloody reprisals carried out mainly in Peking by an expeditionary force of the European powers.

In October 1902 Maude finally took her first furlough[44], long overdue, and little Grace came with her. Inie had a photo of a young Chinese woman about the age of thirty, taken in front of a Chinese building; on the back of the photo is simply written: Grace, 1927, so she must have only been five when she came to Ireland. At the end of their visit they took ship at Genoa on the SS Roon on April 27th 1903. Little Grace would have taken back many memories of the home at Blackrock, and the trip round Europe. Inie was home at the same time convalescing, but perhaps well enough to accompany them to Italy.

Soon after Maude's return Benjamina was transferred to Sang Iong so that the sisters could be together at last. She was doing most of the itinerating work and during part of 1905 she made her headquarters with Miss Garnett at Dong Kau further north in the Ping Nang prefecture. She took her second furlough 1906-1907 and it was during her stay at home that her brother John took ill and died on May 1st 1907. He and

Grace in 1927

Jemima had moved two years before to Powerscourt, a parish in the North. He was only fifty-one and they do not seem to have had any children. Maude came home in October of that year for a much-needed rest and her presence helped to ease the pain of yet another parting. Inie probably travelled home from Japan with Maude, for she was once again ill and exhausted by too much hard work.

Scarcely two years later Miss Burroughs was appealing for help at Sang Iong because Maude's health was failing and she could no longer cope with the boarding school built in memory of Hessie. God called her to eternal rest with Him after only a few days' illness on December 12th 1910.

11   Captain Newcombe [45]

aving followed the heroic lives of her three sisters in China, it is time now to go back to the day, December 3rd 1893, when Inie, aged thirty-six, joined the Salvation Army. Her coming was welcomed by General Booth, who had hopes of taking the Army to China. Indeed, his last words as he lay dying in August

The Salvation Army Logo

1912 were: 'More for the homeless and remember China'. Inie herself was actually in China at that moment. But it was not until 1916 that the Army was able to start work in Northern China.

Meanwhile, Inie underwent some training and worked in the London slums for a few months. With her knowledge of Chinese it would have been natural for her to be sent to help Catherine Hine in Limehouse with her mission to the Chinese there. The meeting between the two women would have been of immense spiritual comfort to both. The following account of Captain Hine's apostolate is taken from the S.A. publication 'God's Army':

> Now, in 1878, a real Army needed a real flag. During the last weekend of September, Catherine Booth presented the

corps at Coventry with the first flag of the Salvation Army. After this, it became the custom for the General and his wife to introduce the 'colours' as they visited each town.

A few years after the Army flag came into existence, Catherine Hine, a Salvationist from the London district of Woolwich, felt she should be a missionary to China. But she was not strong enough for service so far from home. As a Salvation Army officer, her duties were mostly at a desk during the daytime, but the evenings were her own. She decided to devote all her spare time to preaching and visiting the Chinese population of Limehouse, East London.

So that she could communicate, Catherine learned Cantonese and studied Chinese culture. Seamen from the East came to respect her, while the local Chinese residents became her 'children'. She opened a hall for meetings and had her flag emblazoned with Chinese characters. All who attended her meetings heard about the love of Christ.

When one of those converted by Catherine's preaching returned to China, she gave him a flag as a reminder of her mission. At first the people of his village laughed at him and his new-found faith. But he lived a distinctive Christian life, and soon some of those who laughed had become Christians too. A short time later civil war broke out and news came that a band of rebels was approaching the village.

'Now is the time to show us if your teaching is true' said his friends. 'Either this God can save us or he is a lie. Tell us if we can trust him now.'

Inside the man's home hung the flag from Limehouse. He looked at it, wondering what Catherine Hine would have done in such a situation. Then he took it down from the wall and walked out to meet the rebels. He had no idea what he would do when he met them.

As he approached the advancing column, he was amazed to see the leader of the rebels hesitate. He was staring. He recognized the Salvation Army flag! Once he too had been one of Catherine Hine's congregation in London, but he had failed to follow what she taught. However, the sight of the flag brought back a flood of memories and a bond was immediately struck between the two men. The column of rebels marched on, bypassing the village, and the people escaped violence.

After but a few months at work in the London slums, saving souls and feeding the hungry, Inie, the new soldier of Christ, received her marching orders from General Booth. She was to go to India and await the formation of the pioneer party which was to start the work of the Salvation Army in Japan. This was General Booth's response to an appeal received three years earlier as follows:

From 'All the World', September 1892.

The General has received and cordially answered the following letter from Japan:

NEEDS YET UNMET.

Sendai, Japan,
May 7th 1892.

'General Booth, - I convinced that for our country, Salvation Army is very necessary, never save unless there is no Salvation Army, now our country condition is just same as yours, therefore I composed salvation army and had gone to preach Gospel through the country and I got very good result, but Why our country missinaries not like to work in same manner or the army? I think, because they have no the noble spirit as to sacrify their body and spirit for their country men, O my heart never satisfy unless save our country men, so that I wish very very much strong to see you and your army condition and army system, after I return I will compose the army, which works in connection with

General Booth

your army, O General, I wish very strongly to go to you,

please give me a way to go to you, if you cannot give me a way I will go even selling my properties which I wish to use for composing the army, if you please I will bring also my sister. I am now theological student. I am not yet skillful very well to speak, to read, to write in English, but I have very strong conviction about Christianity. I am work every day after lesson among poor. I have two meeting plases and seven very honest helpers: Japanese new papers wrote about our army already often, member of our company increase every weak, and money too, meney churchs love very much our army, please give me answer as soon as you can.

Your true friend,

H.S-----

O God lead me to General Booth, who is my true friend.'

Inie made a great impression on her S.A. comrades in India and they regretted her departure – 'She was just the kind we needed'. But orders came to proceed to Colombo to meet the party coming from London. This was made up of the following officers: Colonel and Mrs. Wright, and their three children, Ensign and Mrs. Paine, Ensign and Mrs. Gosling, Captain Scott Potter, Lieutenant St. John Hart, and Captains Helen Clark, Eva Devonshire and Matilda Hatcher. There was a Farewell Meeting at the City Temple and the Japanese party was pronounced on all sides to be 'extra special' in every sense. By August they had arrived at Colombo (in present day Sri Lanka) and were welcomed by Brigadier Musa Bhai and were reinforced by Major Esu Charan of Gujarati fame, who was taking a three-months fighting furlough in Japan, as well as by Captain Inie Newcombe, 'for eight years at work in China and sister of the martyred missionary there' (although Inie did not get the news until months later).

They travelled to Yokohama in a North German Lloyd Steamer, the SS Hohenzollern, and arrived on September 4th 1895. There they were met by a Japanese Captain Ishigami, who had been converted and trained in America.

They had to spend the night on the ship, having nowhere to go, but the captain refused them any more food. So when they had all put on Japanese dress, Colonel Wright and the two Japanese officers went ashore to find lodgings. There were about two hundred people waiting on the quay. The majority were Japanese. At the sight of their Japanese dress, curiosity soon changed to strong appreciation; but among the few Europeans present, there were distinct indications of a verdict against them. The pioneers accepted the situation and thanked God they were counted worthy!

Unfortunately their first attempt at identification with Japanese culture was misguided. The Japan Advertiser reported:

On September 4th, the first party of English officers of the Salvation Army landed at Yokohama, via Hong Kong. At the last-mentioned port they bought what they thought to be garments worn by the indigenous inhabitants of this country, but the clothes proved to be Japanese night kimonos, and their appearance one bright morning in these clothes naturally created considerable amusement and interest.

After some difficulty, they found a Japanese hotel where the party could stay from the following morning. It was something new for Europeans to turn their backs on the 'Concessions', (districts where Europeans built factories and western-style houses), and seek accommodation in the native quarter of the town. They also had to buy food for their supper, and returned to the ship laden with bread, fish and fruit, which they ate by moonlight, squatting on the deck.

After supper, Colonel Wright and Ensign Gosling went ashore for a look round. They found their way into a part of Yokohama known as 'Blood Town' because of the frequent fights between sailors of all nationalities. Hearing singing inside a pub, they stopped to listen and heard boisterous English voices singing, 'The Salvation Army has come, Oh Lord, have mercy on us, The Salvation Army has come.'

Entering the pub, they said 'Yes, we are here! And we had better pray!' They fell on their knees and had a proper prayer meeting; when they rose from their knees, the Japanese were all standing looking quite frightened – every Britisher, mostly sailors, had disappeared. The next day they were received at the hotel with elaborate bows and prostrations and had their first lesson in eating with chop sticks. The following day they were taken to Tokyo and held their first open-air meeting on September 7th. They had two cornets, one small brass instrument, two concertinas and a drum, and, of course, the flag, which General Booth had presented to them at the Farewell Meeting. It attracted an enormous crowd, lasted two hours and no hostility whatever was shown.

A few weeks later Brigadier Powell arrived with Cadet Loxton from California, who spoke Japanese perfectly, as her mother was a native of the 'Land of the Rising Sun'.

Inie was preparing to go to a meeting when she received the news of Hessie's death. It was to be the first meeting in Tokyo at the YMCA Hall. Colonel Wright had asked her to give her testimony, believing rightly that the novelty of a woman speaker would arouse sympathy. But when she spoke of the news she had just received and of the joy of being counted worthy to suffer and die for Jesus' sake, it went straight to the hearts of her audience, and at two smaller meetings held the same day Colonel Wright had the joy of seeing the first four Japanese come forward seeking salvation.

The pioneering party sought from the beginning to identify themselves with the Japanese, and their first headquarters, the Gochomi house, was outside the 'Foreign Concession' where the Europeans lived. Houses in Japan are built low and flexible to withstand the average of 1,100 earthquake shocks a year.

Inie and the other three women captains lived together in a small house studying the language. Soon Inie took charge of four Japanese women cadets, found a house for them and moved in with them.

One of them knew a little English and could interpret. Kida Shan was 'saved' at one of the meetings. 'A bright, merry little thing', wrote Inie in a report; 'If I make a mistake in Japanese, she will roll over and over in convulsive laughter. Her father wanted to marry her to his adopted son, who would inherit the family business in place of the eldest son who had dedicated his life to God in the Salvation Army. But Kida Shan spoke out bravely and said she also had given her life to God and the Salvation Army; she wished to remain in its ranks and fight for God. So her father has given up the matter and I hope we shall be able to keep her. When she and I go out together, we have been nicknamed "The long and the short of it", and when she stands behind me at a meeting, she is completely hidden. She is our youngest, just seventeen by Japanese counting – only fifteen or sixteen by English.'

The following year, 1897 Inie could write of her progress in the language:

I am getting a little more time for study and making a little progress. At last Sunday's Holiness meeting, I gave my testimony in Japanese, and my teacher says she feels so encouraged because it was so correct. The first part was prepared and corrected beforehand, but the real testimony bit was impromptu, so I felt all the more encouraged that it was understood.

For days at a time I write only Japanese phonetically, with the result that when I take up my pen to write a little English, the spelling comes to grief - I never use English when I can possibly do anything else – and consequently feel very much at a loss when trying to express myself in English.

My own personal experience is that Jesus is enough for me in every difficulty and temptation.

There were changes in the original group. Ensigns Paine and Gosling and their wives returned to England within a few weeks of their arrival. Colonel Wright's eldest daughter developed small pox, so the family was in quarantine for several weeks. In the first year, Captain Scott Potter was taken ill and transferred to America; in the second year, St. John Hart went to Canada and the Wrights went back to England. That left Brigadier Powell and the four women, but he was engaged to an officer in Sweden. He carried on until Colonel and Mrs. Baily arrived from Australia, and then left for Europe. Then in 1900 there arrived Commissioner Bullard, one of the 1882 pioneers of the Army in India, and at once the others realized that he was experienced and understood the Eastern character. But Captain Matilda Hatcher related that he had no idea of the cost of living and reduced their allowance. For a time Inie had to supplement them from her own money until a letter to Mrs. Booth obtained an increase from eight yen a month to thirty! Inie was much older than the other three women, and a born leader, but all her letters at this period show her concern for and appreciation of others. Captain Hatcher remembered her, fifty years later, as 'without doubt, God's gift to our party'.

12   Yokohama

In 1897, so soon after Hessie's death, there came the news that Lucy also had gone home to God. Inie wrote to a friend at the London headquarters of her concern for Aunt Lily, with never a word of her own grief.

> Only last Sunday morning I got a letter telling me another sister had received her call up higher. My darling aunt will feel lonely now in the old home – only one child (Mina) left with her out of the large party that used to fill it. We who are in China and here in Japan, shall miss Lucy's letters, she was our only regular correspondent. My aunt is getting very old and feeble, and seldom feels equal to the exertion of writing. All I have heard about dear Lucy's illness and death is on half a sheet of note-paper – and yet, though my heart does feel hungry to know a little more, and though I realise that this has severed me more than ever from home and friends – yet there is joy in thinking of one more on the golden shore to welcome us up higher. Darling Lucy's whole sympathy was with my work. I could always write to her about it freely, knowing it would only call forth love and sympathy and prayer.[46]

Inie's letter was meant to be private, but her friend made no apology for publishing it in the Mission bulletin 'All the World', saying that she knew the writer too well to think she would care the least what was done with anything belonging to her – her own self included, for that matter – if God's Kingdom could only thereby be helped and extended. Inie ended her letter full of hope and Christian joy:

> We have been having real blessings in the Training Home. Our girls are waking up on the point of Holiness and are going right on into the experience, I believe. I am

longing for the full light to shine in. One by one our Japanese officers are going in for Sanctification. It is glorious to see the change it makes. There is a very real devil to fight in Japan, but, Hallelujah, I have got a gloriously real Saviour, for Whom I fight, and with Whom I am sure of victory, in my own personal experience and in my work. Hallelujah!

At the very time Inie wrote this letter, another missionary lay dying in the Carmelite cloister far away in Lisieux, France. Today St Therese is patroness of the Missions. In her short life of twenty-four years, nine of them spent as an enclosed nun, her love for Jesus had set her free to encompass the world in her apostolate of prayer. In the last throes of her painful illness, all was offered for the salvation of sinners and the spreading of God's Kingdom of love. She faced death's approach calmly, not wishing for anything but God's will. The cessation of her suffering was not to be an Armistice; eternal rest was not for her. 'I want to spend my heaven doing good work on earth. I can't rest as long as there are souls to be saved. I feel my mission is about to begin...'

From her place in heaven Therese would have followed with great interest and sisterly love the ardent apostolic zeal of the Salvation Army. The fact that good Protestants are not allowed to seek the help of the Saints would not have prevented her from lending a heavenly hand. Inie would have puzzled over the mystery herself when Lucy died. Lucy had always supported her sisters by her love and prayers during her life – now that she was truly alive and closer to them, would she be deprived of the consolation of helping them? One suspects that Inie left that problem to Jesus and got on with the work.

When she herself lay dying, it seems she was expecting St James to come for her, as will be related later. This life-long devotion to the apostle and 'brother' of the Lord, who was co-patron of the church where she was confirmed, is significant. His epistle was not popular with the Reformers because of the assertion 'Faith without works is vain'. But the whole epistle would have served as a plan of action for the Salvation Army. 'He who converteth the sinner from the error of his ways shall save a soul from death and shall hide a multitude of sins', and 'If a brother or sister be naked and destitute of daily food and ye give them not those things which are needful to the body; what doth it profit?'

It was truly amazing how the work in Japan spread and prospered during those first years. In the first weeks they had the joy of seeing over sixty souls come forward at meetings to kneel at the penitent-form, although the interpreter with Japanese politeness forbore from translating 'sinners' literally. Twenty-six young men joined the Army as cadets along with several young girls like Kida Shan. A businessman who owned three hundred cottages wanted all his tenants to join under pain of eviction, and had to be restrained from compulsion. So he said he would give them time to consider, and if they did not yield he would raise their rent!

Colonel Wright made a tour of the island by train and threw back numbers of the War Cry out of the train window to the coolies in the fields. Soon Brigadier Powell could report in March 1897: 'We have already six Corps and a Home for discharged prisoners, seventeen Japanese officers, and a paper with a circulation of 2,000'.

As soon as the work was established in Tokyo, the pioneers decided to attack the devil in Yokohama. Inie was one of the officers sent to take charge of the enterprise. The following letter, written by one of the other women captains, Matilda, Eva or Helen, tells the story. Inie was sent to take charge of the Yokohama district soon after the Boarding House was acquired, and must have stayed there two years.

God has blessed our sailors' work at Yokohama. It is just wonderful how the whole thing came into our hands. The Sailors' Boarding House was kept by a saloon keeper, and we have not only got the boarding-house but the saloon as well. I wish I could describe my feelings when I saw our flag go up on the house that had been the biggest and the worst, as well as the most central of all. Such a sensation! The missions practically screamed at us, and the publicans all around held a meeting, at which it was decided to put us down. The missions agreed with the publicans, who said it was not respectable for the Army to keep open so late, so we told them that if they (the publicans) would close earlier, we would do the same; but the Cities of Refuge must be open as long as the Man-Slayer was abroad.

The sailors are so good to us that it is quite useless the publicans hoping to get rid of us. Some of them have gone elsewhere, saying 'All the men go to the Army now, so we must go to Hakodate.'

All the China fleet (European Allies) go to Hakodate for two months in the summer, and now I have had permission to go too. The missionaries here are very kind to us, and I am looking for a suitable house.

The sailors will do just anything for us. The other day the Bishop said 'But what can you two girls do?' I replied, 'We can set the sailors to work to save themselves.' I don't think he quite understood. We only make the Home ready, and the sailors do everything else – wash-up, make beds, and even lead meetings. It is quite funny to see these big men so domesticated. They are like a lot of children playing at housekeeping. But some beautiful work has been done. God has helped us to make a lot of new Leaguers.

One Sunday, not long ago, fifty dollars worth of tobacco went into the sea to the tune of:
'My idols I cast in the sea, My all I return to Thee who gave;
This moment I'm happy and free, from tobacco at last I am
saved.'

The whole community at Yokohama are now in favour of the Salvation Army, and the Bishop told me some very nice things which the Rear Admiral had said about us. I think they will be pleased to find us here when they return from the Russian Seas.[47]

Adjutant and Mrs Ellis arrived to take over the running of the Seamen's Home in 1897, having previously established the Gibraltar Naval and Military Home.

One of the first Japanese officers was Gunpei Yamamuro. He was inspired to translate a collection of Bible stories into colloquial Japanese, which contrasted with the complicated classical language used in previous religious translations. As a result 'The Common People's Gospel' appeared in 1899. It has continually been reprinted, selling over 500 editions, and still remains one of the most useful books to give to new Christians in Japan. It must be remembered that many of those converted at meetings had no knowledge of Christian doctrine, and much of the officers' time was taken up with basic instruction of the converts.

Meanwhile, over in China, Maude and Benjamina continued their devoted work in the schools and evangelization in the villages. For a few years they were together at the Sang Iong mission, then Benso moved to Nangwa. They were both due to come home on furlough at the end of 1896, but it seems that Maude did not go, perhaps because there was no one to replace her. She had adopted a Chinese baby girl whom she brought with her when she took home leave in 1902.

In 1898 a new school building was named the Hessie Newcombe Memorial School, a very moving occasion for the two sisters. They were increasingly on the alert for martyrdom, as alarming reports reached them from the northern provinces. The Boxers were indoctrinating more and more non-Christians with their hatred of the foreign devils and their religion. Their usual method was to hold displays of the elaborate Chinese boxing, which is more like dancing than Western pugilistics, and then raise their audience to mass hysteria with tales of Christian atrocities and their own magical powers and invulnerability. For years the Imperial government had claimed to have outlawed them, but in 1900 they were let loose by the old Empress, infuriated by the incursions of the

Western powers. Thousands of Christians perished in scenes of heroic martyrdom until in August an expeditionary force arrived to suppress the rising with a brutality that was no credit to Europe. In an issue of 'All the World' at the time, Inie is mentioned as:

> ...a most devoted Officer, one of whose sisters was martyred in China three years ago. The Adjutant's two other sisters are now running the risk of sharing the same fate, by heroically refusing to leave their posts and forsake their people at this time of trouble and danger.

 Tokyo and Kozuke District Officer [48]

In February 1900 the Salvation Army in Japan was given a new leader, an experienced officer who had been one of the pioneer party in India and had worked there for eight years. Commissioner Bullard and his wife exchanged the turban and sari for Japanese dress and set about learning another difficult language. They found that two of the original party were already speaking Japanese fluently. This would include Inie, who was still Field Officer at Yokohama.

That summer there was a severe fire which destroyed 4,000 houses, including the S.A. barracks at Yokohama. The houses were built of wood and plaster, able to survive the frequent earth tremors but highly inflammable. There were many nights when they were awakened by the clanging of the fire bells from the high watchtowers

Colonel Bullard gave the following description of a Field Officer's day:

The day is devoted to War Cry selling and delivering copies to regular customers as soon as the fortnightly edition comes out. When a Corps has outposts, these have to be visited at regular intervals. The public inside meeting at night is always preceded by a march and open-air meetings. For this purpose the Soldiers meet at the barracks (usually a rented shop) and march out in the usual manner with the Flag, drum and a large lantern, which is a peculiar feature of the marches in Japan. This lantern is a wooden frame, usually about a yard square, covered with Japanese paper, on which is painted an announcement of the meetings, and, with lighted candles within, it forms a transparency.

The number in the march is usually small, varying from six to twelve. There are generally one or two stops for meetings, which are carried out in the ordinary manner, with songs, prayer and testimonies etc. The Officer's place is always in front to direct the march and lead the singing and he or she is expected to speak at every open-air meeting.

The inside meeting is conducted on the same lines as in the West, except that, on account of having fewer efficient Soldiers, more speaking is required of the Officer. Tuesday is the Soldiers' Meeting; Friday, the Holiness Meeting; the other nights are devoted to Salvation Meetings.

IN THE 'Morning Land'

CAPT. NEWCOMBE
(Sister to the Lady Missionary murdered in China)

Today we have fourteen Corps and nine Outposts, divided into four Districts. Tokio and Kolski Districts being under Adjutant Newcombe, a most devoted Oficer, who formed one of the pioneer party, and, previous to becoming an Officer, was a missionary in China, where one of her sisters was massacred three years ago. The Adjutant's two other sisters are now running the risk of sharing a similar fate by heroically refusing to leave their posts and forsake their people at this time of trouble and danger.

A group of Salvationists

All inside public meetings close with a prayer meeting and an earnest effort to get seekers. They are invited up to the raised area covered with tatami and have to be helped in a simple, patient manner to make their first prayer, since most are only nominally Shintoist or Buddhist and have no religious beliefs. They have no knowledge of Christian truths, and while a few may be favourably disposed towards Christianity, the majority are rather prejudiced against it.

Soon after Colonel Bullard's arrival, he promoted Inie to the rank of Ensign as she continued her busy apostle's life at Yokohama. In a private letter to a friend[49], she gave the following description of one of the Soldiers' Meetings, which shows that the Japanese recruits are of the right quality and full of energy and determination:

Yokohama is going well. I was at a special Soldiers' Meet-ing there the other night. Everyone had to pay five sen admittance. A soldier collected this without any of the false shame natural to him. The moment a man came into the room, before he had time even to sit down, he was greeted with, 'Pay five sen!' This was to provide tea and cake. Later on in the evening when the tea and cake had been enjoyed, another soldier sug-gested, 'We are now eating up ourselves the five sen we paid before; I think we ought to give *another* five sen each to the Captain for the work'. He took his cap and went round and got several yen in a minute or so.

ADJUTANT NEWCOMBE.

To go back to the beginning, how-ever. There was an exhibition of the spoils of the devil's rule laid on a table. There were big whisky bottles, wine cups and bottles, gambling games, rolls of wine accounts etc; one set running over two months amounted to 246 yen 5 sen 2 rin, equal to £24 13s 1½d. Another set in twenty-four days came to 64 yen 5 sen, run up in drink and bad houses. Then there was a collecting book, showing over five yen collected for the building of a Buddhist temple. It was at once suggested that the owner of this should try his hand at collecting for the Salvation temple instead!

Inie then explained the meaning of this exhibition to the Soldiers' meeting, saying,

'This is a picture of the way you served the devil. You can see here what you did for him. Now God has saved you out of his hands. What are you going to do for God? Only ten months of this century are left. What will you do for God before the new one begins?'

Well, I sat by and just kept singing 'Hallelujah' right there, and did long that you could have been there to rejoice with us. Of course the barracks is far too small for them now, but they say themselves, 'Let us go on as we are for some months, and then we will be strong enough to collect for our new barracks and have a proper one'. So we are waiting.

The Rescue Home, Tokyo

On Sunday night the men soldiers have to stand in the street, and go in one by one to give their testimony, and go out again, so as to leave room for the sinners. If they all went in and sat down they would fill the place.

Colonel Bullard thought the time was ripe to open a Rescue Home in Tokyo and so in the middle of 1900 a special issue of the War Cry attacked the licensed brothel quarter, with the result that a number of officers were roughly handled and badly injured. This caused a great sensation and created an agitation on the subject, which stirred the whole of Japan. The newspapers themselves began an attack on the system of vice, and by force rescued a number of girls from brothels where they had been imprisoned. The feeling aroused was so great that the Government had the police regulations revised. Previously, owing to the interpretation of the law, a girl could not give up this life without the consent of the brothel-keeper.

The result was that over the next years, a thousand girls left the brothels and the number of clients decreased. Threats were made against the Salvation Army and the headquarters had to be protected by police. Although accompanied by six policemen, the Chief Secretary, Major Duce, and the War Cry editor, Adjutant Yamamuro, were brutally attacked when going to the help of a poor girl who had appealed to them.

The favourable response and support of the media to the S.A. Rescue work coincided with the emergence of Japan into the international scene. In 1900 the country joined the community of nations and foreigners were allowed to live anywhere in Japan. In 1901 the Emperor issued a proclamation introducing a new era 'in which useless customs and purposeless precedents were to be discarded and justice and righteousness were to become the guide of all actions'. It was noticed that in the repression of the Boxer revolt in August 1900, the Japanese and American contingents behaved less brutally than their European counterparts did.

Salvation Army procession headed by Captain Hatcher – note the high wooden sandals

At Christmas 1900 Inie was again promoted, and as Adjutant Newcombe, was given charge of the

Tokyo and Kozuke districts, which included some eight Corps. Kozuke was a silk-weaving district, one and a half hours by train to the north of Tokyo. By Sept-ember 1901 there were twen-ty corps in Japan with seventy-five fulltime officers and workers. Each corps received an allowance from London HQ but the officers had to live very frugally. Every year during the Self-denial Week they went round collecting funds in the streets and work places.

Such was the pattern of Inie's life in those busy years in the Lord's vineyard. There was scarce time to pray quietly, but daily time was given to her Bible and all was offered to help her Saviour seek and save the lost sheep.

However, after a year of intense work she became ill and allowed herself to be convinced by her superior officers and friends that it was time to take her furlough. That news decided Maude to do the same, for she had not taken her home leave with Benjamina in 1896, and so had been in China for fourteen years. Maude's adopted daughter of course came with her and one can imagine the excitement at Blackrock as Mina got the rooms ready for the two sisters and the little Chinese niece. They felt Aunt Lily's loving presence everywhere in the house. She had died the previous year in May after a short attack of bronchitis. Mina and John were with her at the end.

Inie wrote a long article for the December 1902 issue of 'All the World' describing the work in Japan and the farewells when she left.

All the World, December 1902:

Home again, after seven years' fighting in Japan, and in all the whirl of this first week in London I am asked to give *All the World* readers some information about the fight for Jesus there.

Last days naturally recall first days, and reminiscences of our early warfare were recalled vividly to my mind at my late farewell in Tokyo. As the older Japanese Officers were one by one in their testimonies going back to our first meetings and the impressions made on them at that time, I also remembered the early days, and saw again Staff-Captain Yamamuro, a rather shy youth, a little afraid of making mistakes in English. I recollect vividly the night he told us that he had made up his mind to be a Salvationist. I said something to the effect that we trusted it would be a life-long choice. He did not quite know how to express his purpose in English, but answered he had decided to be a *Cadet* for life!

Thank God, the steadfast purpose so brokenly expressed has been faithfully carried out. A more loyal and devoted Salvationist, I believe, is not to be found in our ranks.

Then there were Yabuki and Takahashi, who have fought with us from the first. Cadet Yabuki came for a special weekend when I was in charge of Yokohama during our first year. We were wakened before six by his voice, as he dealt with somebody about Christ and salvation. He attended three open-air and four inside meetings that day. At each he spoke at great length and in a very high pitch of voice! Between meetings he spent the whole time in personal dealing, and right up till after twelve at night we heard the same tones going on, apparently unwearied, pointing out the way of salvation.

Ensign Minakuchi and his wife also have been very closely associated with me for three years.

My first introduction to the Ensign was when I was in charge of Tokyo 1 Corps, and he arrived, announcing himself as one who had to investigate and see for himself what we were doing. He carried out his plan to the end of the meeting, watching with evident interest while three souls sought salvation. I dealt with him at the close, pointing out that every saved person except himself had helped to get those men saved, and charged him with having let the sinner who had sat beside him go out unsaved when a word might have detained him and led to his salvation. He was deeply impressed, and the next night came again to the meeting accompanied by a youth he had picked up on the way; he led him to the penitent-form, made him kneel down, and then called for some of us to come and help him to Christ, since he had no idea what to say.

Minakuchi came into training, and soon could not only attract the people, but also lead them to Christ. He is very proud of his wife, and a dear brave little warrior she is, knowing English well. I have seen her at a street corner leading an open-air when her husband has been absent, and only a Japanese woman knows what that means! I have known her spend hours in patient *War Cry* selling with her baby strapped on her back.

The Ensign is in very delicate health, showing symptoms of consumption. Please pray for him. We can ill spare him from the front of the battle.

I shall never forget the last goodbye at Shinbashi Station, Tokyo. Such a crowd of Salvationists! They bought platform tickets that they might see the last of me, and as I leant out of the window and saw the Blood-and-Fire Flag waving and listened to the 'Hallelujahs! and 'Amens!' of the dear Japanese comrades, my heart went out to them in gladness and yearning, and I prayed God to strengthen me quickly that I might soon be able to once more take my place among them.

Inie Newcombe, Adjutant.

14 Taking Lucy's Place

As the 20th century dawned, No.25 Mount Merrion Avenue had many empty rooms. Aunt Lily lived peacefully with Mina and the maid. Three years had passed since Benjamina had returned to China. The next sister due for home-leave would be Maude in two years time.

Such was the household when they filled in the forms for the 1901 Census. But very soon after, Aunt Lily took to her bed with a bad attack of Bronchitis. She was 79 and very frail. In spite of Mina's devoted care she slipped away into God's arms on April 19th as John read the prayers for the dying. Only Mina and he were there to represent the nine children she had raised – three had preceded her and three more would follow in the next ten years. The house seemed empty without her loving presence, but she had gone no further than God and He was very near.

Mina had the big house to herself now with fourteen-year-old Sophia Long from Donegal to help with the house-work. The year passed and they began to prepare to welcome Maude the following September. They were looking forward to meeting Maude's little Chinese daughter, Grace.

Inie wrote often about her work and the forthcoming visit of General Booth and the new openness of Japan to other countries. But the work and travelling were exhausting her and she decided to come home with Maude in September 1902. They probably met at Hong Kong and sailed from there to Southampton. Little Grace was delighted with her new aunt from Japan. Inie soon dropped back into Chinese and chatted happily with the little one in her own dialect. The other passengers got much pleasure from Grace's attempts to speak English.

On their arrival in the old home they settled into the familiar surroundings where they had grown up and once more a little child ran merrily up and down the stairs just as they had done. But they had to face the fact that the house, with its four large bedrooms, extensive ground floor and semi-basement, was far too big. When their stay ended Mina would be alone with only young Sophia for company. So a family council was held with John and Jemima and it was decided to look for a smaller house not too far away. There was no hurry as Maude and Grace would be home until the following April and Inie would need more than a year to recover her strength.

The year passed happily and Maude and Grace set off sight-seeing across Europe and took ship for China at Genoa on the S.S. Roon on April 27th 1903.

Inie was still not well enough to return to the tough life of a District Officer in Japan and had to resign herself to spending another year at home with Mina. It would not have been wasted time, for she had only to step into Lucy's shoes and take her place in supporting her missionary sisters and S.A. comrades by her prayer. She had also much scope for her talent as a letter-writer, keeping in touch with family and friends.

Aunt, who had died in her late seventies, had never understood or approved of Inie's life as a Salvationist. St Paul said women should not preach or be over men and Inie was certainly not allowed to wear her uniform in the house, but had to keep it at a friend's house[50]. She learned to tailor her stories of the missions to what was acceptable to her audience. This was also the case when she became a nun, for of all the stories she told at recreation there were none about Japan. Fortunately much was preserved in the Salvation Army archives.

That she was able to adapt to the quiet, slow pace of life after such apostolic activity shows how far she had progressed in the selfless gift of her life to God's will. Her one desire was to live solely for him. So she set about the job in hand, which was convalescence, later taking her share of the housework, social visits to friends and relations and attendance at church with Mina.

During those first years of the 20th Century she heard much talk of the rise of Irish Catholic nationalism. The Gaelic Athletic Association popularised Irish sports such as hurling. The Gaelic League, founded in 1893 to preserve the language, spread rapidly, providing classes in Gaelic. Churches were built from the pennies of the poor and new religious congregations found numerous vocations. All this did little to ruffle the calm waters of 25 Merrion Avenue, Blackrock.

All the while the Dominican Sisters were educating the young women who would live to see Dublin the capital of the Irish Free State. Inie must have spent some of her leisure as she had as a child, watching from her bedroom window the girls on the playing field and the nuns pacing St. Catherine's avenue. If she had made scarcely any progress in understanding and approval of Romish doctrine and devotions, at least she now regarded them as fellow-Christians.

But having painted such a peaceful picture of life in Blackrock, down in the city of Dublin quite a different situation confronted Inie when she felt well enough to visit her comrades at work in the slums.[51] By 1903 there were at least four corps in the city. In those early days of the Salvation Army's arrival in Dublin they had met with a very hostile reception. In the eyes of the slum-dwellers, whose Catholic faith had become a symbol of the fight for freedom, the Salvationists were just another English invasion to be fought with fish-heads, rotten cabbages and stones. Such was the treatment they received at open-air meetings in 1901 that an escort of Royal Irish Constabulary had to flank the march to the open-air stand. It was little better by the time Inie was well enough to visit Dublin comrades, and unless she stayed the night with a friend in the city she would have found it impossible to get back to Blackrock after an evening meeting.

She must have begun to realise that the prejudice of Catholics against Protestants could be as strong as that against Catholicism in which she had grown up. However much she had come to repudiate that prejudice herself, in the eyes of the slum-dwellers of Dublin she was still classed with rich Protestants living off the rents of poor tenant farmers. It was the sheer goodness of the Salvation Army reaching out to the most needy in the slums, in spite of the rough treatment they received, which gradually overcame the prejudice. Their courage in witnessing to their Christian faith in public brought many back to Christ.

Their first recruits revelled in the opposition, although they often risked severe physical violence, with prayer for their only retaliation. As one lad remarked after sustaining a serious head wound from a well-aimed stone: 'Sure, an' Dooblin's a foine place for the Salvation Army, an' all! We have some brave toimes at the open-airs, an' all, Sorr!' The Dublin Salvationists at the turn of the century were experiencing the kind of violent opposition the Army met with in England and on the continent in the early years of its existence. Opposition to William Booth's message was felt as early as 1866 when trails of gunpowder were laid and fired by trouble makers in the old wool-shed where he held meetings in Bethnal Green. Real antagonism grew up in the early 1880s.

Publicans became worried as numbers of their customers joined the Army and gave up drink; some people resented being reminded of their sins and eternal punishment in public; professing Christians objected to the new movement's interpretation of the gospel and, last and not least, many objected to having the peace and quiet of Sunday disturbed by public hymn-singing and brass bands in their streets. They may well be excused at that early date, as musicianship was not all it might have been. Pelting with rotten eggs, mud and stones was common and the police did little to help. Similar opposition was experienced by the Army in other countries for the same reasons. In Connecticut fifty drums were confiscated one by one, only to be used all together in a triumphant procession when later returned. In Newfoundland they were attacked with hatchets and knives when a mob of three hundred attacked women Salvationists. Several were seriously injured in places all over America to which the Army had spread rapidly in the 1880s. In Europe the peaceful Army was being persecuted: many were arrested by the police instead of being protected from their tormentors. Some died a martyr's death as the result of their public witnessing: knocked down and kicked or trampled to death, stabbed, even shot.

With the turn of the century, governments began to understand what the Army was effecting in changing the lives of former criminals and in caring for the poor and the rejects of society. Persecution gave way to tolerance, then respect and finally praise. Only in places like Dublin, where ideologies clashed, did the opposition continue some years longer. National leaders recognised and welcomed the Army's achievements. In 1903 William Booth was officially received at the White House by President Roosevelt, in 1904 by Edward VII in Buckingham Palace and in the following decade, by the Kings of Denmark, Norway and Sweden and the Emperor of Japan.

————— ❖❖❖ —————

15 China? Not yet

By the summer of 1904, Inie was feeling quite her old self and eager to return to full time evangelizing. So the date of her return to Japan was fixed and she made the round of relations and friends to say good-bye, hoping her health would hold out for many more years. John had moved from Monasteroris, to Powerscourt parish in the North near Lough Neagh, the same year that Inie returned to Japan.

Her departure would mean that Mina was once more left alone in the big house. A family council was held and they decided to look for a smaller house not too far away. In 1906 the house they had grown up in with all its memories was sold and Mina set up a welcoming home for her sisters at No. 4, Ashbrook Terrace, Rathgar. Sailing from Cork on the SS Campania, Inie arrived in New York on February 18th 1905. Several meetings had been organised in and around the city in preparation for a special Congress to mark the arrival of George Scott Railton with six women soldiers to start the work of the Salvation Army in the US.A.. Inie spoke at many of the meetings but had to leave before the Congress.

She landed in Yokohama[52] on April 3rd to a warm welcome. After two nights there, catching up on news, she went on to Tokyo on the 5th. The next issue of the War Cry announced her arrival and spoke of her as 'one, rare, devoted person whose whole family is involved in missionary work at their own expense. We believe that, by her joining, Japan Salvation Army has increased in its strength'. There is also a report of the arrival on the 9th of a Colonel and Mrs. Owl or Orwell to start a training programme for officer cadets. So on 10th April there was a grand welcome party for them and Adjutant Newcombe, and also a farewell to two Australian women officers going on home-leave on the 14th: Captain Furnace, who later married a Japanese, and Captain Pearson who served many years in Japan. Only Captain Mattilda Hatcher was left of the original pioneers. Captain Helen Clarke had married Ensign Robson, one of the Australians, and they had worked hard together to establish the Army in the western part of the island at Okayama. But sadly, their first child died. They never got over the grief and left for Australia.

After a short, happy time settling back into Japanese food and dress and meeting old friends, Inie received her appointment as District Commander of Kansai based at Kobe, a port on the west side of the island in the province of Kansi. It was again pioneering work like that of St Paul in Corinth. The population was only nominally Buddhist or Shintoist, so all the meetings had to be backed by prayer that God's grace would touch hearts and open minds to understand this God who had died for them. Even today a century later, only one per cent of Japanese are Christians, though many more have attended Christian schools.

China had for many years been high on General Booth's list of 'Needs not yet met'. An attempt was made during the two years Inie was District Commander of Kobe at least to reconnoitre the terrain. There were at that time many missionaries in China, so it looked hopeful.

It was decided that Commissioner George Scott Railton should go to Japan and from there, go to see the possibilities in China. It was Railton who had led the first expedition to America in 1880, landing in New York wearing the first complete suit of Army uniform. His brave band of soldiers consisted of seven women, only one of whom was over twenty years old. On 10th September 1905 he landed at the port of Kobe. Colonel Brad went aboard to greet him while Adjutant Newcombe and her soldiers were there to welcome him on the quay with their flags. They escorted him to the Seamen's Home where he spent the rest of the day. He crossed over to China to see for himself, but on his return it was decided that

Captain Matilda Hatcher should go there with a Japanese woman officer to see what they could do. Some new law in Chinese ports affecting British and American women led Railton to think the Army could commence rescue work there. The two women were guests of the China Inland Mission and many were willing to help them get started, but without the language it seemed impossible.

It may be wondered why Adjutant Newcombe was not sent since she spoke Chinese. But one must remember that China has two main languages using the same written characters as Japanese but with an entirely different spoken language in the North from that which the Newcombe sisters had learnt in the South. Added to this she had only just returned from two years sick leave. However, the project must have engaged her enthusiasm, concern and, most of all, her prayers.

In 1907 General Booth himself came to Japan and made a tour of all the districts. He was received in audience by the Emperor during the course of his visit. Captain Hatcher received an order to return to Japan to meet the Founder, and she explained to him the difficulties in China: 'Officers must have time to get some knowledge of the Chinese language'. She tells, in her memoirs of Japan, his characteristic reply: ' "Oh! You are worse than Railton. He did say he would go, language or not" and he dismissed me. Outside the door I met Railton and Sawley, both smiling who said, "We came to pick up the pieces!" ' Captain Hatcher continues:

> The next day the dear beloved Founder called me out from a group of officers and said in his inimitable way: 'Are we good friends, Hatcher?' and shook hands heartily and blessed me.

> That closed the Chinese episode and without any more ado I was transferred to Women's Social Work in England to await the opening of China. Nine months later the Founder sent me to India – Blessed be his memory!

What was happening to Inie at this time is not certain. General Booth arrived in Japan on 16th April 1907 and in June a Major Erikson was appointed District Commander of the Kansai area replacing Inie. There is no record of her leaving Japan, perhaps because it was overshadowed by the Founder's visit. She herself, writing twenty years later is not clear about dates. She says of her service in Japan:

> I was about fourteen years in Japan, interrupted by two long furloughs owing to ill health. On my third return home I was faced with the medical decision that return to that work must not be attempted.

Fourteen years would mean that her final return would have been in 1909, her third attempt having taken place before that. However, there is no record of her returning a third time in the Tokyo archives. Her last service in the Far East was in fact the two years she spent in Fujian to replace Benjamina 1911-1913 and it may well be that this was the third attempt she remembered.

When she left Japan in 1907 at the age of fifty, Inie had no idea whether she would find herself once more in her beloved China. All she knew was that her appointment for the immediate future was once again convalescence and the apostolate of prayer. Actually there is no evidence to prove that she did leave Japan in 1907. It is possible that she stayed on some time recovering from illness, since she had sufficient private means to live on. On the other hand she knew that Benjamina had taken home leave the previous October and Maude was due to come home in September 1907. Added to this was the news that John was seriously ill at Powerscourt. If Inie stayed to greet General Booth in April she would have arrived home too late for a final farewell to her brother, who went to God on 1st May 1907. There is also the possibility that she travelled home in the summer, in the care of her sister Maude, arriving on 5th September.

That Inie was able to accept these alternations of apostolic activity and complete rest, without losing her peace of heart shows how faithfully she had lived the donation of herself made at the age of twenty-five.

I realised that my Saviour was offering to undertake himself the work of my sanctification. And with as complete a surrender as I was capable of, I gave myself over into his hands, to do with me what he willed.

These were sad years for Inie. So many of her brothers and sisters had gone ahead to rejoin their parents and Aunt Lily. There had been good news from William in Canada as his six children grew up and the two eldest married. But suddenly in May 1906 tragedy struck when William died of a brain haemorrhage while his daughter Inie was preparing for her wedding in June. Her mother suffered a stroke soon after her husband's death and died in October. The youngest girl, Lucy Lilla, was only sixteen and felt the loss of both parents in one year.

The news of their brother's death was a great grief to Mina and the loss of their sister-in-law so soon after reminded them of their own story. She felt they could repay Aunt Lily's great charity to themselves by inviting Lucy to come and stay with her. She wired her sisters and they agreed. Benjamina came home that October and before definite plans could be made their beloved brother John died after a short illness the following May. A new organ was dedicated to his memory in the church at Monasteroris.

The house was once more full at the end of Benjamina's home-leave because Maude and Inie arrived in September 1907 and Benjamina did not leave until October. One can only imagine their joy and gratitude that God had brought them together once more.

It may have been in 1908 that their niece, Lucy, came from Canada to join Mina and Inie in Rathgar. She soon found a post as governess and became acquainted with all her Irish cousins. So it was that she met the Reverend Godfrey Greene whose late wife had been an Eccles. They married around 1912 and she had three children.

16 Two more years in China

After Aunt Lily died, Maude and Benjamina suggested to their stay-at-home sister that she might like to visit their mission in Fujian. But one thing after another put it off. There was Inie's two years' convalescence, then John's illness and death in 1907. When Maude returned to her post on 28th April 1908, aboard the SS Zeist, the suggestion was probably made that as soon as Inie was well enough, she and Mina should at last make the proposed trip to China. Nothing would have pleased Inie more.

However, one thing after another got in the way and 1909 passed and most of the following year. So it was with great sadness that they learned that yet another sister had gone to God. Maude died on 12th Dec 1910, after only a few days illness, probably a victim of one of the virulent influenza epidemics. They would visit her grave with Benjamina, but she would be as close to them in Ireland as the two brothers and two sisters who had gone before her.

Now this is where God stepped in to change the plans. As far as is known, Benjamina was also a victim of the epidemic and needed a long break at home to recover. She was forty-five at this time and the mission could hardly spare her from the supervision of the schools. There is a brief entry in the CEZMS Roll of Missionaries, that her sister, Inie (former CEZ missionary) offered to go out for two years so that Benjamina could take furlough. Leaving Hong

The Dean's House

Kong on 16th September 1911, Benjamina went directly to Ireland, arriving 8th October.

Inie's offer of help was gladly accepted by the CEZ[53]. She convinced the family doctor that the work would not be strenuous and would not involve open-air preaching. She arrived at Foochow after Benjamina left, but it is quite possible that they met at Hong Kong. Benjamina's boat left there on Sept. 11th, 1911 and Inie arrived at Foochow around Sept.20th. After a short visit to the 'Olives' on Nantai Island she set off on the five days' journey to Sang Iong and kept a careful account of expenses for the coolies who carried her baggage and herself in the old familiar sedan chair: 30 cents for the boat to Nantai, $2.50 for the boat-ride up the river to Ba Sai and $7.80 for the long chair ride up to Sang Iong. The card on which she noted the expenses was providentially used to mount one of the photos she brought to Dolgellau in 1931.

The first to meet her as she entered the village was an excited teenager – it was Grace, so grown up since their last meeting in Dublin. But the tears soon came as she spoke of her foster mother. Maude's passing was still fresh in all their minds – less than a year ago. Aunt Inie put her arm round Grace as they walked together to the long, low house where Maude had lived with her little daughter and latterly Benjamina. They were met by an old friend, Miss Burroughs and two new arrivals, Miss Mander and Miss Wade.

Inie was to take charge of the Hessie Newcombe Memorial School. Earlier in the year it had been closed and the girls sent home when the Revolution swept the country. As no one knew how long the fighting would last, the Consul had once more ordered the withdrawal of the missionaries from the up-country stations to Foochow. The headmen in Kien Ning, once so anti-Christian, begged the missionaries not to go and even appealed to the Viceroy. However, after a few days' fighting in Foochow all was calm in the province, the Republic was a 'fait-accompli' and it was safe for the missionaries to return to their posts. By September when Inie took up her post, the sixty-one girls had returned to the boarding school.

She noticed that many of the younger girls did not have their feet bound in the traditional way to keep them small[54]. Maude had told her about the famous Three Edicts of 1905, which had caused such consternation in Chinese official circles. The old Empress issued an edict abolishing the traditional triennial examinations in Confucian philosophy, which all candidates for the Civil Service had to pass. Instead everyone was ordered to study Western knowledge. The mission schools suddenly became popular owing to the shortage of teachers to set up state schools. It was assumed that all things Western were now approved, including Christianity.

The second edict forbade foot binding and caused no less consternation. The Christians were delighted, but for many years the practice of binding girls' feet from a very young age continued here and there for fear that no-one would want to marry a girl with big feet and she would be left on her parents' hands.

The third edict ordered the setting up of schools for girls – but only for girls with unbound feet. Of course, this immediately raised the status of women in the cities although there was little change in the villages. But in 1911 the new Republic gave the movement full impetus and slogans were chanted 'Men and women are equal'. Many girls refused to submit to arranged marriages and took up a career. The Revolution progressed swiftly and the Emperor, who was only a child, abdicated in 1912. The Republic however, was vast with no lack of warlords with private armies and personal agendas. The President, appointed by Dr. Sun Yat Sen, set the alarm-bells ringing by trying to establish a dynasty and when he proposed to make Confucianism the state religion all the other religious bodies were alarmed. However none were in a position to organize a united protest, except the Chinese Catholics of Tient Sin, the northern port. Here we meet a dynamic little Belgian priest of the missionary congregation founded by St. Vincent de Paul. Father Vincent Lebbe had electrified the Chinese laity of Tient Sin with his preaching in fluent Chinese and organized them to the point where they could publish a highly successful Catholic daily. He succeeded in uniting the main religions of China in protest and the 'Alliance of the Five Religions' soon made sure that full religious freedom was written into the constitution of the Republic.

It is worth noting that not all Catholic missionaries were as enthusiastic about Chinese nationalism. The missions were inextricably linked to European politics: they benefited from Europe's power but suffered from the hatred it engendered. France had the monopoly of patronage of the Catholic missions and resisted any attempt by the Vatican to establish direct diplomatic contact with Peking. In November 1919, the Pope sent out an Apostolic Letter to the whole Catholic Church known as Maximum Illud from its opening words, castigating in no uncertain terms the missionary tactics of the past, which served more to increase the influence of the missionary's home country than the Kingdom of God. It also deplored the fact that native priests were not promoted to the episcopate or positions of responsibility; and last and not least, that so many missionaries and bishops had not even taken the trouble to learn the language of their people. Opposition to the letter among Fr. Lebbe's superiors was fierce on the grounds that the Pope was misled. For his support of Chinese nationalism, Lebbe was exiled to Southern China whose language he did not know and then back to Europe for seven years. But he returned in triumph in 1927 with the first six Chinese bishops appointed by the Pope over the heads of the missionary bishops and given dioceses newly created for them.

In the first year of the Republic there was little change in Sang Iong. Officials were more friendly and Miss Mander reported encouraging visits to the villages where the people were anxious to hear about the western religion. But exciting news was brought up from Foochow by the coolies. Telephone wires and electric lights were appearing everywhere, even on the ancient Bridge of a Thousand Ages. Men were having their pigtails removed – that fashion introduced by the Manchu dynasty was considered anti-Republican. All sorts of hats were being worn and women were trying new hairstyles.

Besides the man-made storm of the revolution there were also the usual fierce storms of wind and rain during Inie's first year back in Sang Iong: the boarding school had been damaged and a new building was being built. The building which housed the Station Class was too badly damaged to be used and had to be entirely rebuilt. By the summer of 1912 it was ready to receive seventeen women for a session of six weeks and in the autumn, twenty-four for three months, and another twenty-four for six weeks. A fifth member of the CEZ team joined them at this time, Miss Seabrook from Tasmania. She and two of the others kept house together in a beautiful wooden house with a shady verandah the whole length of the front. Miss Burroughs and the Newcombes had their own houses in the mission compound.

Box cameras, which had been invented in 1900, were all the rage when George V came to the throne and it was only to be expected that Inie should take a Brownie or Kodak with her on what would almost certainly be her last visit to China. However there is no certain proof that she actually took the photos she brought back. It seems strange that there are none of Grace or the other missionaries. Perhaps these were given to

CEZMS Ladies' residence

Mina. What survives in the little album she brought back are group photos of the Women's and Girls schools and photos of the mission buildings. These may have been taken at the request of the London Head-quarters since she wrote on the back of one 'For Willows'. Probably she got the film developed in Foochow and asked for two prints, keeping one set for herself.

Women's Station Class 1912

Photography was not new in those parts because as early as 1903 Inie had received a snap of Dr. Mary Shire and Nurse Hook of the Foochow CEZ hospital with a group of children from the school for Upper-class Girls. Other photos were sent to her from Sang Iong between 1922 and 1927.

One of the first photos she took was of a group of the Women's Confirmation Class. The Revolution had delayed the Bishop's visit but the ceremony took place soon after Inie's arrival. The fifteen women were photographed sitting on the steps of their school, two of them with their babies on their knees. The sun was in their eyes and there was no way they could be persuaded to smile except one old lady in the back row. There are other photos of groups with the same stolid gloom on all faces. But an old grandmother taken with her two little granddaughters is quite at ease with the camera smiling happily.

Now when the prints arrived back from Foochow (or was it Shanghai?) some time in 1912, Inie thought they were a bit too flimsy to survive. So she looked for some thin card on which to mount them. She had with her or found some postcards with the address of Whiteaway, Laidlaw & Co. printed on one side, meant for mailing orders for goods to Shanghai. Many years later when the photos were removed from the album, the writing on the back in Inie's own hand revealed some interesting details of her stay in Sang Iong. She had used some of the cards as shopping lists or travel accounts. All the expenses of her journey from Foochow Sept. 11th 1911 were meticulously recorded with the interesting addition of the word 'Strike'. There were also the expenses for

a visit to the mission of Dong Kau in the Ping Nan prefecture. Many years before, Rev. Robert Stewart had bought a house in the hope of starting a mission there, but without hope of success. Several years after his death, a CEZ doctor and two nurses

Christians old and young

were sent there in 1902 to start a hospital and this soon opened up the whole district to the Gospel.

Inie would also have made several visits to Kutien to pray in the Memorial Church[55]. Everywhere she was welcomed by the missionaries as one of the pioneers who had gone through persecution and danger to plant the Gospel – but few could understand her reasons for leaving the Society. Although she did not find among them the same bigotry which had so upset her in Dublin, she knew it was wiser not to praise the Catholic missionaries in their hearing. She would have to tread a lonely road into old age when she returned home; it seemed unlikely that she would have the health to continue missionary work even in Dublin. But knowing as she did from experience the joy of receiving mail from home when one is half a world away, she promised to write to all the new and old friends she met during those last years in China. And, Yes, she would pray for them and for China.

Soon enough two happy Christmases in Sang Iong were stored in Inie's memory. There was good news from home:

Benjamina was fit again and looking forward to returning to her beloved China[56]. And better still – Mina had agreed to accompany her for that long delayed visit. The three sisters could spend a few months together and then Mina and Inie would come back together. It was a pity it would be in winter and the situation in Europe was alarming with war clouds on the horizon.

Grace was so excited at the news that she would have three Aunts for Christmas and worked hard at improving her English. The two travellers arrived safely at Foochow in December 1913 and Mina enjoyed the boat trip up the river and the breath-taking scenery. But she viewed with some trepidation the bamboo sedan chair in which she had to ride up the valley to Sang Iong. She got used to being carried by two men and the swaying motion and made several trips by chair over mountain passes in the company of her sisters.

It may well have been after a visit to Maude's grave that one of them remarked that, apart from John, their order of departure for heaven seemed to be 'youngest first' – Charlie, Hessie, Lucy, Maude. Impetuous Inie perhaps said that in that case it was her turn next, if God wanted her. To which Mina could have retorted that, if she went back to singing hymns out-of-doors on cold winter nights, she certainly would be next! This conjecture would explain Inie's famous last words when she heard on her death-bed that Mina was also dying over in Dublin: 'She shouldn't die before me; we girls always die in order of age!'

Yet it was to be Benjamina who caught up with the brothers and sisters who had gone on ahead. Only two years later, at the height of the war in Europe, a cablegram was received at CEZMS headquarters in London on July 26th to say that she was seriously ill and another next day that she had died on July 22nd. The messages were sent on to Ireland. She was fifty years old. 'Come, good and faithful servant, enter into the joy of your Lord.'

 **Fourteen years of struggle**

he next fourteen years of Inie's life are for her personally a time of personal struggle through which she passed safely, due to her long spiritual training in the school of the Salvation Army. She sought the truth with characteristic honesty and courage, prepared to follow her Saviour along mysterious and unfamiliar paths. She has left us her own account of her long road towards the Catholic Church, but very few details of the external circumstances of her life during this period. So before she tells the story in her own words, it will be as well to consult the history books.

In August of 1913, when Inie and Mina were preparing to return home from China, there occurred the Great Transport Strike in Dublin[57]. They must have arrived home in the midst of the upheaval because it lasted until the following Spring. The strike spread and the employers retaliated by locking out all union supporters, causing even more suffering and misery in the slums where the S.A. were carrying on their work of charity. To protect the strikers, the Labour leaders formed a Citizens' Army. In 1912, Asquith, the Prime Minister, had tried to introduce a Home Rule Bill, but it met with fierce opposition from the Protestant North. Although the House of Commons passed it in 1913, the outbreak of the First World War caused the government to suspend the Bill until the end of the war.

On Easter Monday 1916, the Citizens' Army and the Volunteers led an uprising, mainly in Dublin, and seized the General Post Office, the Four Courts and other buildings. But after six days, the leaders agreed to unconditional surrender. Nearly 1,000 women and children had been killed and most of O'Connell Street was in ruins. In May most of the leaders were executed: De Valera was spared because he was

American by birth. In spite of the bloody repression of the 1916 uprising, De Valera was elected leader of the new Sinn Fein Party and in 1919 he set up a government in defiance of British authority.

Soon there began the years of violence – guerrilla warfare and brutal retaliation by the Black and Tans, culminating in Bloody Sunday, 21st Nov. 1920, when the Black and Tans opened fire on a football crowd and the following month burned most of the centre of Cork City.

Lloyd George achieved a cease-fire and proposed a division of Ireland- twenty-six counties in the south and six in the north, each with its own parliament. De Valera opposed the idea, but the Irish delegates accepted the Treaty since the alternative was 'immediate and terrible war.'[58] But, as is still the case, the Irish Republican Army never accepted the division of Ireland and in 1922 Civil War broke out between the Republicans and the Free-Staters and caused untold damage and loss of lives. De Valera called a ceasefire in 1923 and the Free State settled down to work towards peace and prosperity. But the hatred and violence in Northern Ireland continues to fester in spite of the efforts of many good Protestants and Catholics to live in friendship and mutual respect.

Inie and her sister lived throughout these violent years in the outer suburbs of Dublin, but they could not have escaped the general anxiety. The events would have been a constant subject of conversation around them, coloured by the political and religious sympathies of the interlocutors.

One would have liked to know if during these fourteen years Inie took any active part in the work of the Salvation Army, but there is no firm evidence to be had. After the initial difficulties, their work in the slums became established. An early photo of 1901 shows the Belfast Slum Corps with twenty-two soldiers. They did wonderful work relieving the suffering of utterly destitute families with food, clothing, coal and the warmth of Christian love, which made no distinction between Catholic and Protestant. In 1911 a large building, known as Albert Hall, was acquired in Peter Street as a hostel for men and boys. The 119 beds were occupied every night and services were held every Sunday and Wednesday.

Did Inie play any part in all this good work? We can only say that she would have done so if it had at all been possible. Her health and the turmoil of these years would have made it unlikely. However, it would be true to say that she was loyal to the Articles of War, the Salvationists' simple code of belief, to the end. In her personal journey of faith, she followed the Standard of the Cross, emblazoned with the Star of Hope, the Blood of her Saviour and the Fire of the Holy Spirit. God led her to the Catholic Church at the age of seventy and all that went before was a life of total dedication to His service, whether by action or by prayer.

Where did she live during these years? We have seen that Mina lived in Rathgar. She sold Aunt Lily's house in 1906. For some years before 1927, Inie had lived with a friend in the country. When she returned from Wales to settle her affairs in 1931, it was from No.37 Grosvenor Road, Rathgar, that she wrote a letter. This may well have been the home of her sister and cousins, but there is no sure proof. Father Egan may give a clue in a little book he wrote on prayer in 1947, entitled *The House of Peace:*

> I remember hearing a Protestant lady who did much good work among the poor, saying that what she saw on their faces as they came out from Mass, made her long to be a Catholic.

This is how she told the story of those fourteen years:

> With the prospect of living the rest of my life at home, my real difficulties began. Each furlough had found me more and more out of touch with the home church and its activities. The feeling against the Catholic Church, which I encountered wherever I went, was especially objectionable to me. I had come into contact with missionary work of the Catholic Church in China and had greatly admired the

devotion and self-denial manifest in the lives of the missionaries and I simply could not believe in the utter corruption of the Church that had trained and sent out such men. Hostile remarks, which were only too common, hurt me. I felt our Lord was being stabbed in the person of His servants.

After the active life I had lived abroad, I felt the need of some special interest at home, and roused by the feelings I have alluded to, I began secretly to try to find out something definite about the Catholic Church that would justify my favourable opinion. A few novels by Canon Sheehan and other Catholic writers and tracts from the Catholic Truth Society's centre in Abbey Street were all I managed to find. I studied these however, carefully. Soon I began to feel drawn insensibly towards this Church: and then I grew alarmed and drew back and a spiritual struggle began. The more I realized what a strong hold these new ideas had taken, the more I tried to escape.

In this uncertain state of mind, I came across a small book called, The End of Controversy, by Abbé Grou. This I began to read and found to my surprise that at last I had in my hands a clear declaration of what the Catholic Church did believe, by one of its own leaders, instead of the twisted half truths I had hitherto heard from its avowed enemies. I settled down to read and study it and the conclusion I drew in my own mind was that logic was all on the side of the Catholic Church.

From that time, I began to consider what was the real, true idea of the Church of Christ on earth. Up till this time any serious consideration of the claims of the church in which I found myself versus outside bodies, I had quietly in my own mind relegated to the clergy: it was their business, not mine. But now I began to see this *was* my business.

If it was true, as Abbé Grou had maintained, that our Lord had come to establish a visible Church on earth, and had appointed its first leader, and had arranged for the necessary continuation of that leadership, promising definitely that the gates of Hell should not prevail against it, and that to the end of time it would be protected by the ever invisible presence and direction of himself and the Holy Spirit – then came the question: where was that Church today? I had never met it. I turned to my Bible and carefully read and considered all passages in the Gospels, Acts and Epistles relating to this point, and was startled to find how closely New Testament teaching corresponded to Catholic claims. Yes, I found the Catholic Church in the Protestant Bible! And yet, I was a member of a church that was the open and avowed enemy of that Church.

There was no peace for me from that time. A growing conviction, against which I fought hard, took possession of me. Without ever having met a Catholic priest or spoken to a Catholic on the question of religion, I found myself in the grip of the Catholic Church and neither prayer nor effort availed to deliver me. All was dark in my soul. My one prayer was, 'Lord, deliver me from this power that has seized me; let me get back into the old peaceful life where there was no controversy and I could rejoice in knowing I belonged utterly to Christ.' But there was no going back for me, as God was calling me to go on and I was unwilling and afraid and miserable.

At last a crisis came. It was in church at the conclusion of a Communion Service. I suddenly saw that this Protestant Church had become for me an impossibility; I could never again kneel there for Communion or take part in her services. Henceforth for me it was the Catholic Church or nothing. The matter had become simpler. The only question now was, could I become a Catholic? This had to be settled alone with God.

While praying for light, it suddenly came to me, like an inward inspiration, that I had no real doubt about the Catholic Church: that if only my one nearest relation would join with me, there would be neither fear nor hesitation on my part. And then I saw clearly how I was doubting God. I felt He was asking me to adventure out alone with Him; and

I just promised him I would. Instantly there was peace within, where so long there had been darkness and strife. And this inward peace never left me during the troubled weeks that followed, as I set out at once to fulfil my promise.

Within a week I had seen a priest[59], and had been directed by him to a convent for instruction and had told the household where I was living, what I was about to do. I could not explain myself. Only one point was quite clear to me and that was, I had found the Church Our Lord Himself had founded on earth and to which He had given such ample promises of continual protection that I need not fear and must not doubt its teaching; I only longed now to obtain entrance within its fold.

Why such haste? I was asked and I was pressed to wait, to consult authorities on the Protestant side. I had already spent fourteen years since my final return from the mission field during which the Catholic Church had almost entirely engrossed my thoughts and for the last two years I had an ever growing conviction that here, and here alone, was the Church of the New Testament. So at last in loyalty to its head, I was bound to sever all connection with the church in which I had been brought up, chiefly because it was in open and avowed hostility to the One Holy Catholic and Apostolic Church so intimately bound up with Our Lord's life-mission on earth. It remained for me carefully to study Catholic belief from first-hand sources. I got no learned refutation of Protestant errors; but I obtained easily plain dogmatic teaching such as is to be had in the catechism, price 2d, *Faith of our Fathers* and such like, plain reasoned statements of Catholic claims and demands, to which I gave a ready assent. I foresaw difficulty in carrying out some of the demands, but I felt confident that any such difficulty could be met and overcome in the strength of an ever-present Saviour, who was calling me to follow him along this strange and unknown road.

And so I was received into the fold of the Catholic Church; and a deep glad, content reigned in my heart – a content and peace that has deepened and increased as the months have passed in the practice of the Faith that has been God's best gift to me.

Shortly after I had joined the Catholic Church I was talking to a Protestant friend, who was objecting to one thing after another, and at last settled down to the one objection: what was the use of praying in Latin? I had not considered that matter, as I explained to her. It had not been a difficulty to me. I had followed in English with the help of my missal. But her remark led me later to consider and contrast the Protestant Church service and our Catholic Mass and here is the result of my meditation: in the Protestant service, given a good organist, a well-trained choir, carefully chosen hymns and above all a spiritual clergyman and a devout congregation and you have it at its best; and it goes far; I have been deeply moved and spiritually uplifted at some such services.

All these things help to create a spiritual atmosphere; and the atmosphere depends on them; let one or more be absent, everything is dead and you go away disedified. Come to the Catholic Mass, the ordinary every day Low Mass, there is no music, no singing; a little distance down the church only a faint murmur of sound reaches one from the priest who mostly stands facing the altar. Both priest and people are entirely occupied with Someone else whose presence, though invisible, is the great reality of the service. The spiritual atmosphere is there. Christ on the altar makes His own atmosphere. The supreme moment comes. The host is elevated. Amid profound silence every knee is bent, every head bowed and every heart beats as one, in faith and worship, as we render homage to our Saviour King, the God-Man, bodily present in our midst. The Lord is here! My Lord and my God! Blessed is he that cometh in the Name of the Lord! Come let us adore!

Yes, the Real Presence makes all the difference. This is the glorious inheritance of the Catholic Church. The Word made flesh dwells in our tabernacles. All day long the faithful come and meet him there, one by one, and go on their way strengthened.

In conclusion, I ask myself this question. What has the Catholic Church given me that I did not posses as a Protestant and that the Protestant church could never give? First in importance stand the spiritual graces bestowed on us through her sacraments; these, however, are too sacred to be enlarged on here. But besides these very real holy and intimate tokens of the union between the Church and its Head, there are some very distinct gains to which I would like to bear witness.

First then, I would say that I have gained a solid foundation for my Faith and a Divine Authority for my creed and these are totally lacking outside its ranks. Infallibility as claimed by the Catholic Church, resting as it does on the promises of Christ which cannot fail, once grasped, is seen to be the vital necessity of this as of every age. The Church is Divinely protected from teaching error in matters of faith and morals. It has Christ's own warrant and that is enough. Our creed at once becomes real and dominant. Take for instance, two of its items; outside the Church so indefinite and without meaning, while within our ranks they are all powerful. I refer to 'I believe in (a) the Holy Catholic Church and (b) the Communion of Saints.

Faith in the Holy Catholic Church (or in its other more insistent form) the One Holy Catholic and Apostolic Church - what an amount of explanation is required to attempt to assure those outside our Communion, that they still are part of that Church! In my case I know, there remained in the background of my mind, the question 'Where is this Church to be found and do I really belong to it?' Not a safe subject to investigate, I concluded, and left it there. It is different now; I have certainly no need for lengthy explanations: The Catholic Church in its unbroken continuity from its foundation by Christ himself is a visible worldwide historical fact. Thank God I belong to it.

(b) 'The Communion of Saints'. If Protestants spoke the truth, they would confess either that they did not believe or that they knew nothing about it. Another troublesome subject better not meddled with. While seeking the assistance of the prayers of their friends on earth, they condemn as superstition the Catholic practice of seeking help through the prayers of the glorified saints in heaven. Well, I now believe in the Communion of Saints. They are the friends of God and we have abundant proof in our daily experience that God delights to honour their efforts on our behalf. It is much to have gained their friendship and the help of their prayers.

And lastly I remind myself that through the Catholic Church I have gained the Blessed Virgin Mother of God for my own dear mother. I remember how at first I was frightened at using the words, 'Mother of God', having heard them condemned so often. But being certain that as the Church insisted on the constant use of this title of our Blessed Lady, there must be some deep hidden significance worth looking for in it, I naturally turned to the first chapter of St. Luke to see if it threw any light on the matter. I was amply rewarded by what I found.

My first reflection was how easily a preconceived idea may hinder our taking in what otherwise we would hardly fail to see. How familiar this chapter had been to me all my life, yet never before had I noticed the contrast between Gabriel's stem reproof to the aged priest in the temple, and the gentle, respectful, reverential manner in which he delivered his message to the village maiden. But what was even an archangel's reverence in the light of the wonder of his message? Here was the Blessed Trinity actually seeking the co-operation and assistance of this humble maiden, in the glorious work of man's Redemption. Something of the significance of her title 'Mother of God' came to me as I pondered the result of that 'Be it done to me' of her reply.

It stands for the reality of the Incarnation. It was God the Son, the Second Person of the Trinity, who, for nine months, took up His abode in the womb of the Blessed

Virgin and the Word was made flesh and the Word was God
– Holy God, in the crib at Bethlehem; and the Blessed
Mother knelt to adore Him there. And at the end she saw
the Holy God on the cross of Calvary; and the Mother of
God stood by and offered her all to the Father for the
Redemption of us all, as at the beginning, when she had
offered herself. 'Mother of God' is the Church's insistent
proclamation of faith in the God-Man, Christ Jesus.
Mysteries beyond human understanding, but accepted by
faith. Truly our Blessed Lady is ever showing us the fruit of
her womb, Jesus. And so we continue to pray – Holy Mary,
Mother of God – pray for us sinners now and at the hour of
our death, Amen.

18   More to come

After some months of instruction, probably by the Sacred Heart Nuns at Leeson Street, Miss Newcombe was received into the Catholic Church at Rathgar. This suburb was almost entirely Protestant at this time, apart from the servants, whose pennies had built a beautiful church known as The Three Patrons, (i.e. St. Patrick, St.Brigid, and St.Columcille). The rite of the reception of a convert in those days included conditional baptism. This gave rise to a certain righteous indignation on the part of the elderly neophyte as she did not think it at all necessary:

'My father was a clergyman and he knew how to baptize!'

At the time, she was living with Protestant friends whom she helped financially in this way. At the age of three score years and ten, Inie may be excused for thinking of herself as elderly. Captain Hatcher had described her as old twenty years earlier when she left Japan and she had outlived six of her brothers and sisters. So she could be forgiven for looking forward to rejoining them before long in the full flowering of her present spiritual happiness as a Catholic. On the strength of this conviction or hope, Inie began to have some anxiety about what would happen if she suddenly found herself at death's door. Her Protestant hosts had continued to be as friendly as before her conversion, but she knew they would never allow a Catholic priest into their house. So she made up her mind to leave them and find a home with Catholics where she would be certain of the grace of the sacraments at the end. Her first venture was an application to the Dublin Hospice. But the good Sisters regretted that they could not take her in her present state of healthy old age.

It is possible that she found lodging with Catholics or went to live with Mina and her sister-in-law until the idea of

Wales was suggested. Mina was not so opposed to her sister's conversion as most of the family; Inie had had some hopes that she might even follow her. After her reception, Inie began to attend the meetings and the monthly retreats of the Ladies Sodality at Leeson Street. The Sodality was known as The Children of Mary. The nun in charge, Mother Jane Lavery, RSCJ, was, at first, a little disturbed to see among the grand ladies someone so out of step with fashion. For one thing, her most austere flat hat, something akin to the straw-boater of long years gone by, was more than a little out of place; and that queer gray cloak down to her heels was fit company for it. Mother Lavery wondered if she might not be more of a distraction than an edification to the retreatants, despite the fact that, having got as near to the Blessed Sacrament as possible, she was invariably forthwith lost in prayer. Fortunately Mother voiced her misgivings to Miss Mary Angela Boland, her main helper in organising the monthly retreats, and so became acquainted with the story of the old missionary[60].

It was through these retreats that Inie came under the spiritual direction of Father Michael Egan, Superior of the Jesuit house in Leeson Street and also Professor of Mathematics at University College, Dublin. He it was who persuaded her to write an account of her long road to the Catholic Church. Most of it was quoted in the proceeding chapter. But the first paragraph gives a good picture of an old lady on the eve of a great adventure, totally ignorant of where the Lord was about to lead her:

I have been urged to write the story of my conversion to the Catholic Faith. I began more than once but gave up, having found that it takes time to get one's bearings after a spiritual revolution. I would have preferred to wait longer before trying again (it is now just over a year since my reception) but at the age of seventy-one there is not much time to spare, and that is my excuse for making one serious effort to accomplish something of an account of God's dealings with me.

But Fr. Egan found his penitent was far from resigned to 'sitting on the pier with her knitting,' and she once said to him wistfully, 'If the Catholic Church had any use for me in China, I would gladly return there.' He testified that 'Her one desire was to do anything she could for God and souls during what remained to her of life.' But he could hardly have guessed that this seventy-year-old convert, whose health was not of the most robust, would end her days as a Carmelite nun!!!

 The Welsh Mission

W ales was still, from the Catholic point of view, mission territory at the time that God's providence called Inie there. In Penal Times the people had turned to Chapel worship for want of priests and anti-Catholicism had never been as strong there as in Ireland. Since Catholic Emancipation in 1850, Wales had two Catholic dioceses: Menevia with its pro-cathedral at Wrexham, and Newport, which later became the Archdiocese of Cardiff. Breton priests of St. Eugene de Mazenod's congregation worked as missionaries in the north and established parishes; however, they were conscripted by the anti-clerical French government to fight in the First World War and had to return to France.

The parishes of Betys-y-Coed and Pwllheli had fallen into bad times after the withdrawal of the Breton Oblate Fathers and Bishop Mostyn was considering closing the mission[61]. Instead, in 1925 he appointed a young curate from Llandudno as parish priest of Pwllheli, which was a parish covering the Lleyn peninsula south of Caenarfon and ex-

Dolgellau Carmel in 1931, from the South

tended across the foot of Snowdon and beyond Blaenau Ffestiniog. Fr. Leopold Cunningham was Welsh by birth and learned to speak Welsh fluently but at first he met with a lot of hostility from the local Protestants. Perhaps he was too English, but things began to change when they saw him astride the leaky roof of the tin church, mending the holes and turning a wilderness into a tidy vegetable garden. There was no presbytery, but a certain Miss Winefride Noonan, who kept a guest-house in Llandudno, was inspired to uproot herself and bought a house in Pwllheli where she was Father's unofficial house-keeper until retiring to Llandudno in her old age. She gave the house to the parish as a presbytery and is still remembered with affection. Fr. Cunningham suffered a life-threatening illness soon after he arrived and was always in poor health and it was thanks to Miss Noonan that he achieved so much.

A year after his arrival in Pwllheli in 1925, Fr. Cunningham built a more permanent and worthy church, (which served until replaced in the 1980's). In 1931 he was raising funds for a church in Porthmadog. As there were many Irish workers in Wales, his appeals for funds soon reached Dublin and Inie gave a donation. It was suggested to her that she might help in a more permanent way by taking herself and her allowance across the Irish Sea and adding to the number of Father Cunningham's parishioners. She would be able to lodge near the church and have daily Mass and Communion. The idea appealed to her and she quickly made her arrangements and went.

She had often passed through Holyhead in her missionary days and crossed North Wales by train. But staying there through the winter was the big problem as Wales is renowned for its wet, cold weather. It would seem that even before leaving for Pwllheli, she made arrangements to spend the following winter as a boarder with some French nuns at Droitwich. Although no date is available for her arrival in Pwllheli, it is unlikely to have been much before the spring of 1931, the year in which God had turned her life upside down. The only evidence for this assumption is that, until corrected after her entry into Carmel, she mistakenly called Fr. Cunningham's housekeeper, 'Miss Newman.' Surely if she had been there for more than six months, she would have found out her mistake! This did not prevent an affectionate relationship from maturing between them, as is evidenced by her letters, which Miss Noonan gave to the convent after Inie's death.

She mentions also in these letters a Mrs. Jones and her beautiful mother, perhaps with whom she lodged. And there were the church cleaners and flower arrangers who apologized for disturbing her long hours of silent prayer before the Blessed Sacrament. Her invariable answer was always, 'I did not notice you.'

Fr. Cunningham was devoted to his new parishioner and she recognized in him the same selfless devotion that had won her respect and admiration in the Catholic missionaries she had met in China. His mission territory was vast and he thought nothing of going twenty miles in his £5 Austin Seven car to visit one Catholic or to celebrate a House Mass for a family who could not get to the church. He always had time for the children who were won over by his unforgettable smile. He used to pay them to collect seaweed as manure for his garden.

It was to this holy priest that Inie confided her child-hood ambition, now quite impossible, to become a nun. But he amazed her by saying that it might not be as impossible as all that. He had been invited in December 1929, to

Carmel from the North-East

the clothing ceremony of an old lady at the newly-founded Carmelite Monastery which was not far from there, in

Dolgellau, or Dolgelley, as it was called then. So it seemed there was no age-limit in that Order. Further en-quiry would have revealed that the old lady in question was Miss Henrietta Fraser, a convert, aged sixty-three, who had been responsible for the purchase of Fronwnion House and land for the foundation on behalf of the Carmel of Notting Hill, London. She had been accepted as a postulant with certain dispensations from the austerities of the Rule, since her dowry and allowance was a very necessary support for the struggling community.

This custom of taking in sometimes unsuitable subjects under the title of benefactresses has been discontinued, as they were often a distraction and burden on the communities. However, Miss Fraser was an exception and, although somewhat eccentric, proved her vocation and died a Carmelite at the age of eighty-eight. In July 1930, she and her allowance were transferred to the new foundation at Bridell, near Cardigan and remained there as Sister Magdalen of Jesus until her death in 1954. She was much loved by her community.

Inie wanted to attend the Ladies' Retreat in Dublin at the beginning of August, so Fr. Cunningham suggested that she spend a few days at Dolgellau on the way to Holyhead. She could visit the convent to see if God would open a door for her there. His sister and niece were visiting him at the time, so it was arranged that they should drive her down to save all the many changes on the railway. Miss Noonan would go with them and take a present for the nuns in honour of the Feast of Our Lady of Mount Carmel and also a letter from Father, supporting Inie's plea.

On that momentous drive through the summer beauty of the Welsh mountains, Inie must have felt herself carried by God's providence. After lunch at the Criterion Hotel[62] in the town square where she was to stay, they went to the convent for Vespers, which according to Carmelite custom, was entirely chanted on one note. They were shown to the parlour and spoke to the prioress through a curtained grille. The conversation turned to Father's endeavours to build another church at Porthmadog and the fine vegetables they had brought from his garden. An interview was requested for Miss Newcombe the next day and they settled her in her hotel room and drove back to Pwllheli.

The next day, Friday, 17th July, Mother Mary of Carmel, the prioress, began a letter to Fr. Cunningham:

J.M.J.

Friday, July 17th 1931   Carmel, Dolgelley,
                                                                   N.Wales

Dear Father Cunningham,
Regina Decor Carmeli, ora pro nobis.
Many thanks for your kind thought in sending us a gift for Our Lady's Feast. We are truly grateful. I was very pleased indeed to see your sister and niece and the old lady, who, I am sure, *is* a real saint. You speak of her desire to enter religion. I have not spoken with her yet so I have no idea. It sometimes happens that God sends a soul to end her life in Religion but not very often.

There are so many reasons against it that I cannot hold out real hopes for her. The hours – the food – the cold (worst) – the Divine Office – the regular life – the inability to be as a little child and health is a big factor for her I should say. It does sometimes happen that an old person can receive a religious vocation in spite of all the reasons against. She has not been to see me yet – today has been very wet and quite impossible for the long walk uphill. We are having a Clothing Ceremony on Thursday August 13th (Sr. Mary of Trust) and we should be very pleased indeed if you and your sister and any friends would care to come – we hope you will do so. Vespers will be at 2:30 after which his Lordship the Bishop of Menevia will preach the sermon and perform the Ceremony.

May I ask your prayers for our postulant and indeed for all the community and myself. With all our gratitude, I assure you of our poor prayers always.

> I am yours very sincerely in Our Lord,
> Sr. Mary of Carmel

PS: Saturday 18th,

Dear Father Cunningham,

I have just seen dear Miss Newcombe. She is certainly a perfect saint but she has no vocation to Carmel and I think she realizes this now quite well.

> Yours very sincerely in Our Lord,
> Sr. Mary of Carmel

Inie returned to her hotel room after the interview with the Mother Prioress that Saturday afternoon not a little dazed. So near and yet so far.... Mother had been so kind and understanding – an Australian convert who said she had tried several denominations before becoming an Anglican and coming to England to join some Anglican Sisters. Then one day she had known quite clearly and suddenly that the Catholic Church was for her the only way... But she was quite firm that it would be unwise for Inie to attempt the impossible at her age... So next day she made up her mind to try her luck (or God's providence) at Droitwich, where the French nuns had a less austere rule. She wrote to tell Father Cunningham:

> Central Hotel,
> Sunday 19th July

Dear Father Cunningham,

Many thanks for your letter, also for the gloves which I very stupidly forgot to remove. I am quite comfortable here and the weather has been fairly good. Some rain most days but generally fine. I have been to the convent every morning; it is a climb but I take it quietly and manage all right - returning is easy enough.

Now about your suggestion: The idea of the Convent life in general has always appealed to me from my childhood when from my bedroom window I overlooked the enclosure of a Dominican convent and saw the Sisters pacing up and down, and whenever I considered the question of entering the

Catholic Church I looked forward to entering a convent; but I had no particular drawing to one more than another, practically knowing nothing of any of them; also my age was, I realized, a real obstacle. The foreign mission field, work among pagans, or for that at home, was the only real vocation I felt outside the one desire of my heart to live wholly and entirely for God, drawing ever nearer and nearer to Him. All that I have known of Carmel realizes the ideal; alas that it is an ideal beyond my reach! I went to see the Mother yesterday and had a long talk with her - and we both agreed it could not be for me. I realized I would only be a charge on their hands unless a miracle was wrought in my physical frame - my strength would not hold out a week.

I had a bad time after I came back. It seemed as if I had had a peep into a heaven on earth, but the door was closed to me. However the sky is clear again. I go to Droitwich on the 24th D.V. and I will see there, if God opens a door for me. I am staying till the 31st and return by way of Dolgelley and Avonwen to Holyhead and Ireland.

I shall be sure to let you know the result. I thank you from my heart for the interest you have taken in me. As also for our beautiful drive. Please remember me to Miss Newman. Also to Mrs. Jones. I hope I shall not forget her and her beautiful mother.

Yours very sincerely,
Inie Newcombe

However, God had other plans up His sleeve and on Tuesday, Inie received a letter from the French nuns who regretted that they must cancel her stay with them that winter because they had decided to return to France. Inie remembered Our Lord's parables about persistence in prayer and wrote another letter to Mother Mary of Carmel, which she gave to the extern Sister after Mass at the convent on Wednesday. Her letter to Fr. Cunningham tells the story:

July 22nd Wednesday
Central Hotel, Dolgelley

Dear Father Cunningham,

Thank you very much for your very kind letter and your suggestion. Strange to say, the day you wrote I had had a letter from Droitwich that morning - telling me that the convent there was about to be closed and the Sisters were all returning to France.

After praying over the matter, I realized that I was now free to tell Rev. Mother here how much I longed to enter Carmel if it were at all possible and I spent the morning writing to her, enclosing the letter from Droitwich. I brought the letter and gave it in on Tuesday morning after Mass, and coming back here found your letter! I decided I would not consider it till I had seen the Mother again and I went this afternoon and we talked the matter fully out. She thinks that it is quite possible, as you said, but an exceptional case like mine she could not decide and advised me, if I still desired the life, which she fully explained to me, to write fully to the Rev. Mother Prioress in London. She gave me the address and I have written to her and asked if she could arrange an interview any day before the 31st, when I am due to return to Ireland. I could go to London and see her, taking the night train back to Holyhead.

So you see where I am. I am waiting on here till I get her answer. Once more a door, and such a door, seems to be opening for me far beyond anything I had dared hope for.

I shall write again when I get an answer to my letter, which will probably not be till Saturday evening. Should I get a favourable reply, I shall always think I owe it to you and your remark when you hinted it might not be impossible, which gave me courage to apply.

I shall write later to Mrs. Jones and thank her for her very liberal offer. Indeed I can never thank you enough for your interest in my fate.

With kind regards to Miss Newman, I remain
                    Very sincerely yours,
                            Inie Newcombe.

July 27ᵗʰ Monday
Central Hotel, Dolgelly

Dear Father Cunningham,

I am leaving here Wednesday morning for London to see Rev. Mother Prioress Thursday afternoon about 2:50. Please remember me in prayer that the Lord's will for me may be accomplished in me and by me.

I am counting on your prayers, Yours,

I. Newcombe.

Please remember me to Miss Newman and also to Mrs. Jones.

At the Carmel of Notting Hill, from which Dolgellau had been founded, Inie was shown to the parlour and spoke to the prioress, Mother Mary of Jesus, and told her of her hopes and her long road to the Catholic Faith and of her desire to be of service to her Lord. Mother encouraged her and gave her consent. She wrote to the prioress of Dolgellau: 'You must accept her. She is a perfect saint. I love her. And you must give her my name Mary of Jesus.'

Mother Mary of Jesus at Dolgellau

That same evening Inie caught the train for Holyhead and began her retreat with the Ladies of the Sodality next day. She wrote to Fr. Cunningham to tell him the good news:

No date - August ?   37 Grosvenor Road,
                                       Rathgar.

Dear Father Cunningham,

Your letter arrived just the morning I was leaving Dolgelly for London and it put courage into me. When we only want God's will it keeps one calm.

It is all arranged. The Rev. Mother Prioress was quite satisfied to accept me and I returned straight here to make arrangements for moving. I hope to be ready early in September.

It is very wonderful how God has led me on and opened His way for me. I shall indeed remember Pwllheli and pray often for you and your work there.

I feel my soul has truly found a resting place and when God has called and opened the way He will give the necessary strength both of body and soul. I count on your prayers.

Remember me to Miss Newman. You will come to see me sometimes in Dolgelly. Also to Mrs. Jones. I hope to write later, but I felt I must let you know the result.

Yours very sincerely, I. Newcombe.

In Dublin she met Fr. Egan once more. They had kept touch by letter while she was in Wales and in answer to her news that she had been accepted to enter Carmel he had written to her: 'Aren't you a hero! The word "heroine" does not cover it all!' During the retreat, naturally, they discussed the subject. Father said to her:

You say that the Prioress put all the hardships of the life before you; I doubt if she did. She told you of the austerities.

'Yes,' she replied, 'and they did not deter me; at my time of life, I would just as soon fast as eat.'

'Quite so,' I said, 'but the real hardship is this: all your life you have been accustomed to do what you felt was right and go where you thought fit. But if you enter there you will be a child. "Come here and go there, do this and do that," without any consultation of you.'

'But,' she countered, 'won't God give me the grace for that?'

'I'm sure He will,' I replied, 'but that is what He'll want to give you the grace for, not the austerities.'

Inie plainly had her mind made up, and at last, when her affairs in Dublin were all settled, she said good-bye to Mina and her close friends. They could not understand what she was doing except that it was God's mysterious will. It would not be long at their age before the eternal reunion in heaven.

A week before leaving Dublin she wrote to Miss Noonan, who had been such a support to her all through the great adventure:

> Sept. 1st 1931
> 37 Grosvenor Road,
> Rathgar, Dublin.

My dear Miss Newman,

The Peace of Jesus!

That is the Peace I have been enjoying these weeks. I am sure you have wondered why I never wrote, but I have been very busy and I was waiting till I could give definite news of my entering. The date is now fixed: it is this day week, Tuesday, 8th Sept., Our Lady's Birthday. Is it not lovely? I was received into the Church nearly four years ago on Dec. 10th, within the Octave of her Immaculate Conception and now she bestows her royal bounty on me - birthday honours for poor unworthy me, opening the door of Carmel for me to enter. I am travelling Monday 7th, but do not reach Dolgelly till evening – 6:17 p.m. – the train is due. I sleep the night with the extern Sisters and enter on the 8th. I have not yet received my name in religion. The Rev. Mother Prioress of Notting Hill is to choose it.

I am sure you will all remember me on the 8th, Father Cunningham, yourself and Mrs. Jones. I am going to pray specially for Mr. Jones that he may get the gift of the Faith.

Just think when next you come to Dolgelly I shall be inside. I was reading an account of the ceremony on the 15th Aug., and saw Father Cunningham's name among the visitors and I expected you and your niece were also there.

God has been very good to me, and in my joy in the service I am entering on, I shall always connect it with that lovely drive when first I heard that there was a possibility of entering.

Yours very sincerely,
Inie Newcombe.

 Sister Mary of Jesus

September 6, 1931 was a tearful day for seventy-four year old Inie as she said goodbye to Mina and her close friends. The next morning she caught the early ferry at Kingstown and crossed the Irish Sea to her Promised Land. The train from Holyhead to Dolgellau passed through Avonwen near Pwllheli and some of her friends were very probably at the station to wish her God's blessing on such a momentous journey. The railway no longer goes as far as Dolgellau but the Cambrian Coast Line is one of the most beautiful in the country and one has constantly to choose between the view of the sea on one side and that of the mountains on the other. After changing at Barmouth, the

weary traveller would soon have seen the rugged crown of the mountain range of Cader Idris – Arthur's Chair – to the south, with the austere lines of the saddle between the two side peaks. It was to be her last view of the mountain, for she was to live her last years on its lower slopes, too close to see the summit. The sun does not rise above Cader's 2,000 feet during January and it is always a joy when the first winter sunshine falls on the monastery.

The train arrived at the little station of Dolgelley in the evening of Monday, September 7th, and the taxi was waiting in the yard. At that time the local sweep ran the taxi as a sideline and on one occasion the previous year, he had been called to the convent to drive the Mother Foundress, Mother Mary of Jesus, to the station. He had obviously fitted the driving in between two chimney jobs. The extern Sister was horrified at his sooty face and shirtsleeves. But Mother was delighted and beamed at the black face smiling at her from the driving seat and exclaimed in her French accent, 'Oh! I love him!' Maybe he recounted the incident to Inie as they crossed the town and drove up Cader Road.

The extern, Sister Mary of the Holy Child, welcomed her, gave her a meal, and found somewhere for her to sleep in the very cramped extern quarters of those early days; but she was used to adapting herself to circumstances and must have been very tired and dazed.

The next day at Mass in the chapel, she gave herself wholly to God in the spirit of her life-long trust that He would give her the grace for whatever lay ahead. Father Green was the chaplain and Parish priest until just a few months before Inie died.

Then the solemn moment arrived and those heavy gates, which blocked the end of the wide path between the side of the house and the high enclosure wall, were to open for her. Two keys grated in the double locks and the gates swung ajar to reveal the beautiful panorama of the North Cader Range with its green wooded heights and the valley below. So great was the slope of the garden that the enclosure wall did nothing to obscure the view.

However, the group of nuns waiting to welcome her immediately caught Inie's attention. They threw back the long veils which had covered their faces while the gate was opened and embraced her warmly. Besides the Prioress, Mother Mary of Carmel, whom she had met in the parlour, there was the subprioress, Sister Mary Assumpta, looking even less than her twenty-three years. They led the postulant along the narrow path around to the front of the house, through what had been the front door, through a beautiful octagonal room and into the nun's choir. There she realized that she was at last on the other side of the iron grille, which had so fascinated her every time she had seen it from the chapel side, to left of the altar, knowing that behind it the nuns were living their life of prayer.

After a moment of greeting her Master in the Tabernacle on the other side of the grille, they took her to her room and dressed her in the postulant's black dress and bonnet. This was no problem for she had always loved the Salvation Army bonnet. She also knew all about discipline and obeying orders - for one did not argue with General Booth. She had adapted herself in turn to Indian, Chinese, and Japanese culture and customs and more recently, to many Catholic customs, which were so strange after a lifetime as a Protestant. Latin was child's play after so many oriental languages, especially when considering the complications of the Japanese courtesy vocabulary. She knew her Psalms by heart and soon recognized them in Latin as old friends. While it is true that Catholics of that epoch viewed Bible reading with suspicion as something that Protestants did, the monastic daily prayer of the Divine Office was pure Scripture: the Psalms were recited at the Hours throughout the day and long lessons from the Old and New Testaments were read at Matins and Mass, all of which was in Latin, of course, but the Scriptures were also read in English at meals.

There were no musical settings for the Office to be learned and practiced because St. Teresa of Avila, in her Constitutions of 1567, had laid down that everything should be sung monotone or recited, 'for the Lord will be pleased if some time remains so that the Sisters may earn their livelihood.' (But to compensate, they would spent their Sunday and feast day recreations singing hymns and traditional songs with Sr. Winefride providing improvised parts). Nowadays the sisters are allowed to sing parts of the Divine Office to simple tones.

After supper, which was more festive that night as it was Our Lady's birthday, Mother Prioress led the postulant to the recreation room where the Sisters had gathered, and introduced her by her new name, Sister Mary of Jesus, which was chosen by the Mother Foundress herself. The Sisters were sitting on the floor, making a cushion from their long thick habits, but Sister Mary of Jesus was given a stool.

The talk soon turned to the telegram which had announced the death that morning of Sister Beatrice, one of the beloved old French Sisters, who had come from Paris for the foundation of the Carmel of Notting Hill from which so many British Carmels were founded. As the Sisters reminisced about her and their own novitiate days at Notting Hill, the newcomer remembered her recent interview there, which had opened Carmel's door to her.

There were ten other Sisters in the community at that time, only two years after the foundation. There was a postulant dressed like Inie, Sister Mary of the Cross, who had entered in May, and a novice, Sister Mary of Trust, wearing the Carmelite habit but with a big white veil fastened into her scapular at the back. The two lay sisters also wore white veils: Sister Joanna from the Isle of Barra and Sister Agnes from Lancashire. They were still in the period of their three years of temporary vows and so were still under the novice mistress, who was also the Prioress. Then there were three young choir Sisters also still in temporary vows, but wearing black veils: Sister Winefride, Sister Mary of the Blessed Sacrament, and Sister Teresa of St. Joseph. The last of these had been sent from the recently founded Carmel at Bridell near Cardigan to take on the office of Bursar or Depositrix. Sister Mary Assumpta had made her final vows in 1930, as she had entered at Notting Hill at the age of seventeen.

Mother Mary of Carmel was forty, but the only other one in the community over the age of twenty-eight was Sister Mary of the Epiphany, who had entered the Notting Hill Carmel in 1928; she was then thirty-eight and very set in her ways. She is remembered as often declaring: 'I've always done it this way and this is how I'm going to do it.' Mother Mary of Carmel was her devoted nurse in their old age, feeding her and pushing her round the garden in an antiquated wheelchair until her own sudden death, which was followed in a few weeks by that of her old Sister patient, whom she had nursed so lovingly.

So this was the community that welcomed the new old postulant, all but two of whom were to be with her in formation. She took the last place with her simple humility, joining in the housework with the others. She was given the job of helping in the refectory - accent on the first syllable in monastic pronunciation! This entailed the eternal cycle of laying and clearing the long tables, setting out the heavy pottery soup bowls and filling the water jugs. All was done with great carefulness. One of the young choir Sisters was appointed as her 'angel' to instruct her in all the details of monastic life, and she was always very obedient and grateful for any instruction or correction.

Her excellent memory stood her in good stead, for just two weeks after her arrival the whole timetable changed. The long monastic fast season began on September 14th, a period of greater austerity, which lasted until Easter Sunday. The Sisters got up an hour later at 6:00 am. and dinner was at 11:00 am. instead of 10:00 am. There was no breakfast, only a drink of hot sweetened water; but they insisted that Inie take a cup of tea and something to eat, and also continue the prescribed siesta, which was part of the summer horarium. These and other dispensations were, for her, more of a mortification than the austerities themselves, but Mother Mary of Carmel wisely insisted and she obeyed.

At Pwllheli, her friends were wondering how she was coping and Father Cunningham wrote to offer any little extras she might need.

Mother wrote back and Sister put in a letter for Miss Noonan:

Sept. 27, 1931

JMJT

Carmelite Convent,
Dolgelly.

My dear Miss Newman,

Jesus!

I have been wanting to send you a few lines to thank you and Father Cunningham for that lovely drive. I was rather dazed that day and could not express what I felt. But indeed I was and am most grateful. It was such a relief to be taken care of and saved all the trouble of waiting and changes. I would have asked permission to write before this, but I was waiting, thinking you would like to hear how I was getting on.

Even yet it is difficult for me to say. I find my age a continual handicap and at first I got worried and troubled because I could not be just like the others and also because I found myself so dependent on the consideration of others. I found it very humiliating - but humiliation is a good school and I must 'in my humiliation keep patience.' If only Our Mother does not get tired of such a useless postulant and send me away, I shall, I am sure, learn more and more the secret of living in and with Our Lord.

I have told you of my difficulties, not because I am disheartened, for I am not; but that you and Father C. may pray hard for me that I may not disappoint my Lord who has called me here.

Ever gratefully yours,
Inie Newcombe.

Sept. 28th 1931

JMJT

Carmel Dolgelley N. Wales.

Dear Father Cunningham,

Jesus!

I waited until today to reply to your kind letter for I wanted to be able to tell you that we had received your wonderful marrows. You are certainly to be congratulated on the result of your labours, and we, I do assure you, are more than grateful to have them. It was extra kind of you to think of sending money for sugar to make jam. We purchased the sugar and some ginger today and Miss Newcombe has told me a most excellent way of making marrow jam, so we are going to make some at once.

Many thanks for your kindness. Miss Newcombe does remarkably well for her age but she feels it very much that she cannot do more. Please pray for her.

With kindest regards and assuring you of our humble prayer always.

Please pray for us all.

Yours very sincerely in Our Lord,
Sr. Mary of Carmel.

P.S. I have come to the conclusion that the things as extras which will help dear Miss Newcombe most are eggs and tea - the other things which she needs in that way we are able to provide for her. If you feel at any time that you wish to help her these would be a great help, but, please Father, remember that we shall give them to her in any case, so do not feel bound.

In October, Sister Teresa of St. Joseph pronounced her perpetual vows of Poverty, Chastity and Obedience with her hands between those of her prioress. It was done privately in the Chapter Room with only the professed Sisters present. The three years of temporary vows had only come into force in 1918 and the first vows still retained their solemnity, being followed by a public ceremony when the Sister received the black veil, often from the hands of the Bishop himself. Later the Church insisted that the profession of vows should be made in a public ceremony.

In November there was such a public ceremony when Sister Mary of the Cross put on the Carmelite habit. Inie knew that the next postulant to take this step would be herself, God so willing. So she looked on with wonder as Sister came down that day arrayed in a wedding dress and veil and was conducted to the public chapel by little bridesmaids. The chapel was packed with Catholics from Wrexham and many local non-Catholics. Around 1995 an old lady recalled that her mother always took her to the 'weddings at the Convent,' as they called it. After the habit had been blessed, the 'bride' returned through the enclosure gates and reappeared in the choir wearing the habit, having had her hair cut short. The wedding dress custom died out later and today the ceremony is private.

Christmas came and our postulant loved every moment of the Carmelite customs. They wrote verses to well-known tunes to sing at recreation along with endless carols. Cribs were set up and fasting had a truce for a few days. The rejoicing went on until the week after Epiphany. Soon the day was fixed for her Clothing, March 17, St. Patrick's Day, and Inie was measured for her habit. Invitations were sent out. Bishop Francis Vaughan had to ask his Vicar General, Rev. Michael McGrath to preside in his place. During the week before the Clothing, two more of the foundation stones of the community made their final vows: Sister Mary of the Blessed Sacrament on the 12th and Sr. Joanna on 14th March 1932.

Many a tear was shed in the crowded chapel on St. Patrick's Day as they saw the radiant old face with its thousand wrinkles framed by a wedding veil. Someone was heard to say, 'I hope they will be kind to the poor old lady!' Mother Mary of Carmel later remarked that it was more a case of, 'Would the poor old lady be kind to herself?'

After a hymn and prayers the Vicar General questioned the postulant as to her intentions and aspirations. She replied in a firm voice that she hoped to persevere with the help of God's grace and the prayers of her Sisters. A homily followed and then her brown Carmelite habit and white cloak, which were placed on a table near the altar, were blessed.

Then began for Inie the long walk back down the narrow aisle between the tightly packed rows of friends and well-wishers, many of whom were in tears. She was helped with her veil and bridal dress as she stepped outside on that cold March day and passed through the enclosure gates. There the Sisters met her and gave her an arm until they arrived safely in the inner sacristy. Her habit had arrived by a shorter route, having been passed through the sacristy turn, a revolving cupboard, which connected the inner and extern sacristies. Although the public chapel and the nuns' choir were  adjacent rooms until 1960, they were separated by the grille through which the Sisters could see the altar and receive Holy Communion without being seen by the congregation. So it was a good ten minutes before the novice reappeared in choir dressed in her brown habit and white cloak.

There a carpet filled the middle of the floor edged with fresh flowers. During the litany, which followed, she lay face down with her arms out-stretched as a sign of her desire to be ever more closely configured to her crucified Saviour.

Once the ceremony was over, Sister Mary of Jesus would have been able to greet her friends in the parlour and perhaps she wore a sprig of shamrock pinned to her scapular? That evening, tired, but so happy, another surprise awaited her. All the poets of the Carmelite community had composed verses to celebrate her Clothing and sang the lyrics to popular tunes. The following, written for a later novice, to the tune of The Wearing of the Green are given here as an example of Carmelite verses:

Oh! Sisters dear, and did you hear the news that's going round,
At Dolgelley's dear Carmel a happy bride is found.
And we, on Mary's mountain in her blest silent town
Are rejoicing for one Sister more is wearing of the Brown.

I met with Christ's dear Mother and she took me by the hand,
And she said,' How does my country fare, and how does she
    stand?
She's the most delightful country all the world up and down,
And every day she sends recruits for the wearing of the Brown.

21 Novitiate Days

For the first days the new novice needed help putting on her habit and adjusting the headdress of the linen toque and white cotton veil. She also had help at night to learn how to fold everything up correctly and balance the pile on the stool at the end of her bed. Hanging it up on a hook behind the door was a later innovation frowned upon in those days.

In May Sister Winefride made her final vows. She was a convert like Inie and her nurse during her final illness. About nine years before she celebrated her 100th birthday she wrote down all her memories of Sister Mary of Jesus and it is to her and to Sister Mary Assumpta that we owe many of the stories of her childhood and missionary life in China. Mother Mary of Carmel herself wrote the following description of her elderly novice:

> In the noviciate she humbly took her place as the last in the community. Her sight was rapidly failing from very early in her year as a novice, (1932-33), but she always took her turn at reading in the refectory and noviciate, very laboriously preparing the prescribed passages with the aid of a large magnifying glass. Sewing soon became impossible for her, and she used to knit stockings for the novices and shawls for the Sisters until her sight was almost gone. Picking up her stitches was a frequent occupation for her neighbours at recreation.

She loved the Divine Office very dearly, and understood the Latin almost by instinct. As her hearing grew worse, she had to accept having to sit silent; but she always said the Psalms under her breath. She spent every possible moment in learning the Psalms by heart in Latin, preparing for the time when she would be completely blind. She calmly accepted this cross, which was a particularly heavy one for her, as she loved the Office. She was a great reader, with a mind of great breadth and depth, ever seeking to go deeper into the great truths of Revelation. She could never know enough about the Catholic Faith and was increasingly grateful for it.

At recreation she was always full of fun. She had many stories of life on the mission and elsewhere. Her memory was prodigious and her telling of Bible stories was inimitable. Her Sisters always asked her for a story for she was very entertaining and always willing to please others.

The two following mission stories are recounted just as Sr. Winefride remembered them sixty years later:

Some of Sister's stories, told beautifully as they were, were often in demand and often repeated. As for instance, the story of the missionary who asked a rickshaw man to take him to a certain village. The man and all the other rickshaw men refused. At last one of them said that the devil lived on that road, and only on condition that the missionary would repeat the Holy Name of Jesus non-stop all the way, would he take him.

The missionary agreed but the poor man was worn out long before they reached the village because every time he stopped to get his breath the rickshaw man stopped and refused to move until the prayer started again. Needless to say, the missionaries, touched as they were by the good man's faith, soon found another way to that village!

There was another story, which we could never hear too often, and, tragic though it was, when the end came it made us more than smile:

There was a young missionary who was preparing to go home on leave, taking with him his wife and children. Instead of going down to the port by road, he decided to go by the river, which meant shooting the rapids. He would do all the business and then send for the family who would come by road. Alas! There was an accident and the poor man was drowned. The widow, apparently rather helpless by nature, and very shocked by the tragedy, was quite unable to cope with the situation. So the Missionary Society took the family in hand, collected the fare home, packed them up, arranged for someone to meet them at the other end and saw them off. The poor widow did not know what she would do after that... At this point, Sister Mary of Jesus would pause, look very seriously round at us all - then - in a very solemn voice - every word drawn out.... 'But the Lord knew what *He* would do,' another pause,.. 'The ship was wrecked in the Red Sea...and they were ALL DROWNED - And that was the end of it!'

However, it must not be assumed from this that all was easy for her. She wrote the following revealing lines to Father Cunningham in November 1931:

Dear Father Cunningham,

Jesus!

Thank you for your kind letter - it helped me as I tried to put it into practice. I feel I am beginning to get light in and on this new life so different to anything I have ever before experienced. New habits may be difficult to acquire, but what of that when it is God who asks them of us, and even if things were more difficult, I would not exchange the life here for anything the outer world could offer.

I wonder if you and Miss Newman will be coming to the Clothing, (of Sister Mary of the Cross), and if so shall I have a chance of seeing you in the parlour? You would need to come early to visit me, as the parlour will be occupied after the ceremony.

With kindest regards to Miss Newman, I remain

Yours sincerely,
Sr. Mary of Jesus.

Several other events marked her year as a novice. In June, Sister Mary of the Holy Child entered the enclosure as a postulant. She had been the Extern Sister since the foundation, looking after the visitors and doing the shopping. Each monastery had one or more of these valiant Sisters, since the enclosure laws for the nuns were very strict. They lived outside the enclosure, made only simple vows or promises and were dressed in black with a bonnet instead of a veil. Nowadays they wear the Carmelite habit, make vows like the other Sisters and come into the enclosure for meals and recreation.

Sister Mary was replaced as Extern Sister by Sister Bridget and in August, Sister Josephine came to join her and share the extern duties. Mother Mary of Carmel loved the Turn Sisters, as they were called, and went to great lengths in her consideration for their well-being.

In July there was a visit from Bishop Vaughan and he spoke to the whole community about the wonderful event of the Eucharistic Congress in Dublin, which he had attended, and about the spiritual uplift it had been for Ireland.

In August Sister Mary of Trust made her first vows for three years and Sister Mary of Jesus wrote and recited or sang these verses:

Sister of Trust, still forward go,
Trusting in Him who loves you so,
Trusting in her, Our Lady's grace,
Until you meet them face to face.

We greet you here, Oh Sister dear,
And pray that you may persevere,
And ever trusting ever prove
The depth and height of Jesus' love.

And so this day you gladly start
Afresh, bound closer to His Heart,

Nearer and closer day and night
Until trust deepens into sight.

From your humble and devoted Sister Mary of Jesus.

Pray for me.

In December, Sister Mary of the Cross made her first
vows and two days later, another of the foundation Sisters,
Mary of the Epiphany, made her final vows. These were
private ceremonies but there would have been a public
ceremony soon after when the Bishop officiated at the giving
of the black veil to Sister Mary of the Cross. But Bishop
Vaughan was ill and it was put off until January 1933. Even
then he was still not well enough and delegated Father Green,
the chaplain and parish priest of Dolgelley to preside in his
place.

Sister Mary of the Cross was sent to the Carmel of Bridell,
near Cardigan, in September. She returned to Dolgellau in
1976, when Bridell Carmel closed. Many Carmels were being
founded in Britain in the years between the two World Wars
and the foundress, Mother Mary of Jesus, had permission to
move Sisters to form the new communities.

Three letters of Christmas 1932 have been preserved.

Dec. 21st 1932

+J.M.J

Carmel, Dolgelley

Dear Miss Noonan, [63]

Gloria in excelsis Deo!
The little cards take you all the loving wishes and prayers of
Carmel for Christmas and the New Year. May I ask if you
would kindly give to good Mrs. Jones the little card I enclose.

These little gifts have been made by the Sisters for you all.

With loving wishes and prayers,
Yours very sincerely in Our Lord
Sister Mary of Carmel.

P.S.   Sr. Mary of Jesus is well and sends much love and all possible good wishes for Christmas. Perhaps she will write a line herself.

+

J.M.J.

My dear Miss Noonan,

Our Mother has kindly asked me to add a few lines wishing you and Father Cunningham a happy Christmas and New Year. All the blessings of our Infant King for you and yours.

Yours sincerely,
Sr. Mary of Jesus.

Dec. 29th 1932   +

J.M.J.

Dear Miss Noonan,

0 Mary, I trust thee.

Very many thanks for your kind wishes and the lovely parcel. It was such a surprise. I had not thought I should get any parcel and I could not think who would be sending me one. You see I know no one on this side of the Channel except you and Fr. Cunningham. Such lovely chocolates and a cake enough to go round us all - it was so kind of you to think of sending it.

We have had a very good Christmas here and we hear that God is working among the people here opening their hearts and dispelling old prejudices. Please tell Father that I constantly pray for his intentions and shall continue to do so.

Please remember me to Mr. and Mrs. Jones. All kind wishes for a holy happy New Year for them. May God bless them.

Now I am afraid I must finish up. Wishing you and Father Cunningham a truly happy prosperous New Year in the best sense of the word. All the best gifts our Father has for His children.

I remain yours sincerely,

Sr. Mary of Jesus.

Holy Year 1933

C hrist Our Lord, the Son of God, died on the Cross to redeem the world in the year 33 AD, and although there may have been some inaccuracy in the computing of the year, it has been the custom of the Catholic Church to commemorate the centenary of our redemption each century with a Holy Year. This custom began spontaneously from the grass-roots level in the Early Middle Ages, when the Pope realized that enormous crowds of pilgrims were coming to Rome in those particular years, and so the Holy Year celebrations became a fixture. So in 1933 Bishop Vaughan led a Welsh Pilgrimage to Rome and later came to tell his Carmelites about it.

The year was also very special for Sister Mary of Jesus, for it was in March of that year that she was due to make her vows and be totally dedicated to God like the nuns she had seen from her window in her childhood. The date was fixed for March 25th, the Feast of the Annunciation, and she prepared for it by a retreat of ten days. This meant extra hours of prayer and solitude and the wise guidance of Mother Mary of Carmel. It was the custom for the prioress to address her homily personally to the novice at the weekly Chapter meeting on three successive weeks before the date of her vows. The subject was the three vows she would make of Poverty, Chastity and Obedience and the whole community listening with her would renew their own dedication.

The vows are called the Evangelical Counsels because they are a response to Our Lord's invitation: 'If you would be perfect, go sell all you possess and give it to the poor and come and follow Me.' Not everyone is called to do it literally but all Christians are called to follow Christ and his teaching in whatever walk of life he has placed them.

There was another formality that Sister Mary of Jesus had to go through some time before the day of her vows. This was the Canonical Examination. The Bishop or his delegate, in this case Father Green, came to examine the novice on her motives and on her understanding of what she was undertaking. The interview had to take place outside the enclosure to make sure that the novice was not under any constraint or coercion. She was allowed to have her photograph taken while outside and we are fortunate that an admirer of the old missionary did, in fact, take several photographs of her and the old negatives still produce good pictures[64]. We owe them to the wife of the local Catholic, Mr. Ellis, author of a history of Dolgellau[65]. They were the first converts to Catholicism after the monastery was founded in 1929. In some of the photos, Sister is wearing a black veil over her white novice veil; this was allowed, as there would be no chance of a photograph after her vows.

The great day arrived at last. Surrounded by her Sisters, Inie knelt before her prioress and read her vows in a firm voice. Her joined hands were held between those of Mother Mary of Carmel as a sign both of the obedience she promised and also as a sign of the support which she could always count on - the support of God, coming to her through her prioress, who would help her to fulfil her vows. After the simple ceremony she embraced each of her Sisters. The ceremony took place in the nuns' choir with no congregation in the chapel, as there was no room in the house for a separate Chapter Room. For the rest of the day, Sister wore a crown of roses, and during the Divine Office she took the leading part as hebdomadary, as was the custom. The austerities of Lent were, of course, relaxed for the day.

On May 24th, the last of the foundation Sisters, Sister Agnes, made her final Vows. She lived to celebrate the

Diamond Jubilee of the foundation and even appeared on television in 1989. When old age had made her repetitious and single-minded, she greeted everyone with the same enquiry, 'What will it be like when I meet Jesus?' Her Sisters would patiently reply, 'Wait and see!' However, the doctors, nurses, and workmen were left perplexed and thoughtful.

The public Veiling ceremony for Sister Mary of Jesus had to be put off until June 28th because the Bishop was not free till then and he insisted on presiding[66]. So, early in June, invitations were sent out.

Father Cunningham replied on the back of a post card of Portmadoc Church, which was to be named Church of the Holy Redeemer in honour of the Holy Year.

St. Joseph's, Pwllheli
14th June 1933

Dear Mother Superior,

Thank you very much for the great privilege of the invitation to the ceremony of giving the Black Veil to Sister Mary of Jesus. If you do not expect an extraordinary sermon, I will be much honoured, only hoping it will not be extraordinarily bad.

We will come the evening before and if there is no one else to say the ceremony Mass, I would find it easier to say that Mass and preach; but if some one else is to say the Mass I can say Mass some other time. The post card is of Portmadoc Church in its present state. It is nearly ready for opening. Would you please ask Sister to double the number of small altar breads each week until further notice. Also to post each week on Thursday. The children have a Communion Mass on Saturdays. Please excuse

Yours truly,
L. Cunningham.

The Bishop arrived on the eve of the ceremony, and after signing the accounts, he spoke to the whole community in the parlour. The next day, everyone was up early. Father Green's

Mass at 6.30 am. was followed by the Bishop's Mass at 7:00 am. At 8:00 am. Father Cunningham celebrated the ceremony Mass and preached on the text:

> Is it a small thing unto you that the God of Israel has spared you from all the peoples and joined you to Himself that you should serve Him in the service of the tabernacle, and should stand before the congregation of the people and minister to Him? (Numbers 16:9)

The Bishop blessed the veil at the end of Mass and passed it through to where Sister Mary of Jesus was kneeling just inside the choir near the grille. Afterwards she would have gone to the parlour wearing the black veil of a professed Carmelite to greet the people.

That afternoon the Bishop officiated at the clothing of Sister Mary of the Holy Child. In October an older postulant came to join them in the novitiate. Sister Mary of the Angels, Inez Falkner, was forty-six when she entered and although she was a very quiet, prayerful person, she had a great gift for singing and entertaining the Sisters at recreation. She died of cancer, which she had borne with patient heroism, and shares Sister Mary of Jesus' last resting place in the Dolgellau cemetery.

23   1934-1935

Bishop Francis Vaughan was one of Inie's admirers to the extent that he kept a little snap of her in his pocket-book until his death. Indeed he was very fond of all his Carmelites, having asked for and obtained from Mother Mary of Jesus no less than four Carmels in his diocese of Menevia – Dolgellau, Bridell, Llandovery and Presteigne, of which only Dolgellau survives today.

In March 1934 he visited Dolgellau and told the Sisters about the Holy Year pilgrimage to Rome. The Sisters told him about the relic of St. Thérèse of Lisieux which had been sent to them by the Pope. To the Sisters' dismay he begged them to exchange it with the one he had. They gave it with as much good grace as possible! Their own relic was returned to them along with the photo of Inie after the Bishop's death.

Another postulant entered and although she did not stay long, it raised the problem of where to put a fourteenth person in the old house already stretched to its limits. The ground floor was entirely taken up by the chapel and choir, sacristy, kitchen and refectory. The small wing known as the Annexe, built at the foundation, had two rooms downstairs, one of which was used for noviciate lessons and community recreation, but probably it also had a bed in it. The other room was Sr. Mary of Jesus' cell.[67] That was where Sr. Winefride nursed her in her last illness and it is now the Oratory where the Blessed Sacrament is reserved - she would have been happy to know that. There were three small rooms upstairs in the Annexe and seven in the old house but several of these had to be used as the occupant's workroom. Then there was Bethlehem, the old stone cottage in the vegetable garden, about a hundred yards from the house. This housed the laundry, Chapter room and the altar-bread baking room, while upstairs there were three small rooms. It was connected to the house by a corrugated iron corridor against the enclosure wall known as the Tin Cloister. For some time Sr. Winefride, Sr. Agnes and another valiant soul slept down there and had to negotiate the Tin Cloister after the last office each night at 10 pm. on cold winter nights with a candle which invariably blew out. This was banned by the Bishop and the attic of the house had to be divided up into compartments, neither soundproof nor draught-proof, to house the overflow. The big problem was lack of funds. But the Sisters had not expected an easy life and put up with the inconveniences cheerfully.

Bethlehem

There was much to pray for in 1934 and God has mysterious ways of letting his enclosed pray-ers know about the great needs of the world. It was the height of the Depression, known in England as the Slump; Hitler was turning Germany against the Jews and preparing the horrors of another war; Japan had invaded China and the rise of nationalism and materialism had brought a decline in the work of the Salvation Army in Japan. The notice board of most convents was loaded with requests for the Sisters' prayers and one Sister was heard to murmur: 'They seem to know what we are here for!'

Inie did her best to take her share of the work, but there were more and more things she could not do or was not allowed to and it was all offered up, for she was always a missioner, eager to pray and suffer to bring more souls to God. Some time in 1934 she fell and sprained her ankle and before it was completely better, she fell again and broke her wrist. It must have happened on one of the important feasts of the Church, perhaps Ascension Day or Pentecost, when the Sisters took turns all day praying before the Blessed Sacrament. Sister had gone down to the laundry in Bethlehem with her washing and had allowed herself plenty of time before her appointed hour of prayer. But alas, she slipped in the laundry and when she picked herself up, realized that her wrist was probably broken. There was nobody in Bethlehem at the time, so she fastened up the arm somehow and got herself back to the house. She went straight to choir and took the place of the Sister who had been there for the previous hour without saying a word. This precious time alone with her Lord was more important than a mere broken wrist. They had travelled so far together and one can only guess at the degree of holiness to which God had raised her.

Another office followed immediately on her hour of prayer, perhaps Vespers and Benediction. Sr. Winefride noticed that Sister had difficulty holding her book and as soon as the office was finished she had the wrist strapped up. The doctor attended to it, but unfortunately the fracture was badly set and when healed had to be re-broken and reset, with much pain for her old bones.

In October that year the Sisters heard that a second Welsh Carmel was to be founded at Llandovery, a small town in Carmarthenshire. Two days after that good news came the less good news that Sr Teresa of St Joseph, Inie's 'angel', was to go at once to Notting Hill to join the founding group and become the first prioress of Llandovery Carmel. The parting must have been hard for her and she used to tell her new community the stories Inie told about her childhood and the missions. It is from Llandovery that we owe the delightful detail that some of the congregation used to wait outside the church to see the nine little Newcombe children arrive for the Sunday service.

In March 1935 the Sisters heard that their bishop was very ill and on the 13th they received a telegram to say that he had died. He had been devoted to his Carmels and so was his successor, Bishop McGrath, although in a different way as will be seen.

Sister Mary of Jesus was still needing a lot of help, because her arm was not completely healed. Mother Mary of Carmel and all the Sisters were very attentive to her needs, but on March 31st she had a bad fall and broke her leg. There is no mention of her going to hospital, but the pain so weakened her that it was thought advisable that she should receive the Sacrament of the Sick, in those days called the Last Anointing. She was, after all seventy-seven. Father Green came into the enclosure to administer the sacrament and all the Sisters knelt in her room or in the corridor. It was a very beautiful ceremony and gave her all the grace she needed to bear the pain.

For weeks she lay helpless in bed, nursed by Sr. Winefride. The fracture healed at last and she was able to walk with a stick. She no longer had enough sight to read but the Sisters loved to read to her. There was little she could do in the way of work now; that gave her more time for prayer.

Having a missionary in the community certainly gave greater impetus to the Sisters' prayer for the missions and missionaries. The apostolic dimension of prayer is one of the hallmarks of Carmelite spirituality and inspired Saint Teresa of Avila to found her reformed monasteries in the sixteenth century. However, the arrival of Inie in the community at Dolgellau was not their first contact with China and Japan. Sr. Mary Assumpta's aunt loved to travel and sent postcards to her niece from the Far East. Sr. Winefride's mother, Grace Richey, was also a 'globe-trotter', with a sister living on a rubber plantation in Malaysia and friends in Tokyo and Shanghai. On a post-card of Mount Fujiyama dated 1931 she wrote: 'Saw this in all perfection yesterday. Am with a friend in Tokyo. I go to Aunt Winnie at the end of the month - Love, Mother.'

After the Japanese invasion of China in September 1931, Mrs. Richey's visits would have brought news of the war for the Sisters' prayers. Inie would probably have gone to the parlour with Sr. Winefride to meet her.

So while China and Japan were at war, far away in Wales a little old nun was praying and offering all her physical sufferings as a prayer for peace. She saw no newspapers and heard no radio news; but she lived the words her Saviour had taught us to say - OUR FATHER - THY KINGDOM COME - deliver us from the evil of war, and hatred between children of the same Father, her beloved Chinese and Japanese brothers and sisters.

24 **The last year**

There is an old Irish joke in the form of a proverb: Live each day as if it was your last ... and one day you will be right!

Certainly Sister Mary of Jesus must have begun 1936 with the resolution of doing her very best for God's glory, because it might very well be her last year. She was so frail and crippled by her last fall. It took her so long to get from her cell to the Choir and refectory with the help of postulant Norah, and so much of what was said had to be repeated to her. She had plenty of time now to pray in the solitude of her little room or the Oratory. When Mother Mary of Carmel said how sorry she was to have to leave her alone so long, she would say: 'Don't worry, Mother, I am never alone. God is always with me; I am quite happy'. At recreation she was her usual cheerful self, always ready to tell a story.

Soon after the New Year, the subject of Sister's final vows was proposed to the community and they voted in the traditional manner with black and white beans. When all the white beans were put in the white box and the black ones in the black box that meant a unanimous agreement, and the date was fixed for March 25th, feast of the Annunciation. A few weeks beforehand Sister had once more to pass a canonical examination and this time Bishop McGrath delegated Father

Malachy Lynch for this formality. He was a Carmelite friar from Aberystwyth who later became very well known in Catholic circles as the re-founder of Aylesford Priory in Kent. It had been the first Carmelite foundation in England in the Middle Ages and the Order was able to buy it back in 1949. Fr. Malachy's great faith and zeal built it up into the well-known and loved pilgrimage centre it is today.

The ceremony of final vows was held quite privately in those days with only the community present. After the Second Vatican Council the Church insisted that, as these were public and ecclesial vows they should therefore be made in public in the presence of the Bishop or his delegate. Another change is that the black veil is not given until final vows, as this is a sign that the Sister has become a member of the chapter of the monastery, with the right and duty of voting at the election of the prioress and her council every three years and for the reception of new members.

In that solemn moment when she read her vows with her hands between those of Mother Mary of Carmel, Inie must have gathered up her whole life to offer it to God. He had led her along many mysterious paths, her faithful Friend and Guide. Some would call it an 'Eleventh Hour' vocation, but she certainly had not been standing idly all day like the vineyard workers in the Gospel parable (Matt. 20:1) waiting to be hired. She had lived her life to the full in God's service and there was still work to be done saving souls by her prayer and suffering.

At this time there was some anxiety in the community tempered by a lot of trust in God's providence. As has been explained, the house was too small and there was no money to build the necessary extension. Bishop McGrath was well aware of the poverty of the four Carmels in his diocese and very concerned about their future. When Mother Mary of Carmel wrote to him asking his permission to accept two postulants, he replied asking how they expected to support a further influx of nuns on their already meagre resources. He said frankly that he was very uneasy about their financial position - as were all the bishops in general and Dolgelley was not a place to offer much support. He suggested that if they decided to take the two postulants, they should ask Notting Hill Carmel for financial help. 'If not', he wrote, ''tis a matter between you and your Bursar whether you can maintain the new ones. The whole business bristles with financial difficulties and 'twere desirable that something satisfactory be settled'.

Mother wrote in great distress to Mother Mary of Jesus at Notting Hill: 'He wants everything in his diocese to be on a financially safe footing. Our Carmelite trust in God even to apparent foolishness is not the outlook which he takes when dealing with finance.'

Mother Mary of Jesus sent back the letter with her reply written between the lines: 'My beloved child, all will be well. I will help you always in your needs. Tell the Bishop and I will also write to him.'

So Mother Mary of Carmel was able to tell the community that 'Beloved Mother' as they always called her, was making them a long-term loan to finance the much-needed extension to the house. They were able to take one of the two aspirants, Norah Poole, who became devoted to old Sister Mary of Jesus. She spent hours reading to her and inherited her profession crucifix.

The most urgent need to be met by building was to provide better living space for the two extern Sisters and some accommodation for a guest. Owing to the slope of the ground it was not thought possible to extend the house by a new wing, although in 1960 this was attempted successfully. However, the two sacristies and the end of the chapel had been all one storey only, built on to the side of the house very solidly, with a flat roof. So the plan was to raise two more storeys above them to match the rest of the old house. Thus there would be no need to dig foundations and life could continue as usual underneath. The Bishop called to see Mother on July 10th after the funeral of Judge Ellis and approved the plans drawn up by the architect, Mr. Foulkes Jones. The contract with Mr. Arthur Jones, the builder, was signed on July 30th and a month later building began.

At first the building did not interfere much with the regular life of the nuns. Sister Winefride could hear a lot of noise above her head as she went about her duties in the sacristy and the people had to pick their way between piles of bricks to get to the chapel door. It is doubtful whether Inie ever saw the workmen although all the Sisters prayed constantly for their safety. Disturbance and dust came later when the new gable was linked to the old and what had been a window became a door as great stone blocks were hammered out of the thick walls to make new openings. The building was probably far from completed during Inie's lifetime, but she rejoiced at the thought that some of the hardship borne by the community would be alleviated.

As her general health began to deteriorate rapidly, Sister kept more and more to the solitude of her cell, coming with great difficulty to Holy Mass each day.

In October she made a special effort to join the others at the daily recitation of the Rosary. It was the time of the Spanish Civil War when hundreds of priests and nuns were martyred for their faith. Welsh lads who had gone to Spain in good faith to fight for the workers' rights, had been disillusioned by the mob violence they saw.

One night at the beginning of November, Inie became ill and the doctor was called. He said there was no immediate danger but her poor old body was completely worn out and she could not live much longer. Father Thompson, the new chaplain gave her the Sacrament of the Sick and brought her Holy Communion each day. She was too weak to leave her bed and depended gratefully on Sr. Winefride's nursing. She knew she was going to God and longed for the day. Even at this stage she still recited the Office of Compline each evening by heart, with the right psalms for each day. One day Sr. Winefride found her weeping. 'They said they would come for me three days ago - and they have not come!' 'Who are they, Sister?' 'St. Joseph and St. James; they said they would come for me.' Vision or hallucination? Who is to say? And which of the two and possibly three St. Jameses we shall never know until that blessed day when God answers all our questions!

As November wore on it became obvious that the end was not far off. When she was no longer able to receive Holy Communion, Father Thompson insisted on coming all the same to bless her with the Sacred Host although it meant a long walk past the building site. Then one day a letter arrived from Dublin to say that her older sister, Mina, was dying. Inie's indignant reaction surprised the Sisters: 'She should not die before me! We always die in order of age...Youngest first!' Mina did, in fact, wait her turn On November 28th Inie had a bad turn and the Sisters gathered round her bed to recite the prayers for the dying. Sister Winefride and Mother stayed with her all that night and at 5.20 next morning she passed silently away, without any struggle. It was just a peaceful falling asleep in the Lord.

It was the first Sunday of Advent, November 29th 1936. She was 79 years old.

Her funeral was celebrated on Wednesday December 2nd by the chaplain, Father Thompson, assisted by Fathers Cunningham, Malachy Lynch, and Basil Rowlands, parish priest of Machynlleth. Her grave in Dolgellau cemetery has a stone cross which must have been paid for by friends, since the Sisters usually have only a simple wooden cross. Many years later, Sr. Winefride's brother, Michael Richey, told how he had been sent by the stonemason for whom he worked before beginning his naval career, to correct an error of one letter in the inscription. The Bishop's permission had to be obtained for him to enter the enclosure, since the headstone was kept there until the correction was made. Perhaps the builder's men set it up when that was done? The inscription, which is scarcely legible today, reads:

SOROR MARIA A JESU Die 5 Aug. 1857 nata Die 25
Martii 1933 Monacha Professa Die 29 Nov. 1936 obiit.

All these years derive their fruitfulness from her
consecration to God in Baptism and achieved their final
consummation in her five years as a Carmelite. The hymn she
sang at her Confirmation, '0 Jesus, I have promised to serve
Thee to the end', sum up that whole life of faithful service.
The last two verses make a fitting end to this story of a
vocation.

O Jesus, Thou hast promised,
To all who follow Thee,
That where Thou art in glory,
There shall Thy servant be;
And Jesus, I have promised
To serve Thee to the end,
0 give me grace to follow,
My Master and my Friend.

0 let me see Thy footprints,
And in them plant my own;
My hope to follow duly
Is in Thy strength alone.
0 guide me, call me, draw me,
Uphold me to the end,
And then in heaven receive me,
My Saviour and my Friend.

John E. Bode (1816-1874)

Epilogue

When Inie died on November 29, 1936, among the saints who welcomed her into God's heaven would surely have been the two Carmelites, Denis and Redemptus, whose martyrdom in the Far East is commemorated that day. But St. Dominic would very likely have claimed first place, since Inie's conversion and vocation owed so much to his sons and daughters in the Order of Preachers.

In one of her letters to Father Cunningham, dated 19th July 1931, she writes: 'The idea of convent life in general has always appealed to me from my childhood, when from my bedroom window I overlooked the enclosure of a Dominican convent and saw the Sisters pacing up and down, and whenever I considered the question of entering the Catholic Church, I looked forward to entering a convent; but I had no particular drawing to one more than another, knowing practically nothing of any of them; also my age was a real obstacle.'

The convent Inie speaks of was and still is, the Dominican Convent and Girls' School of Sion Hill. The school playing fields were immediately behind Aunt Lily's house in Merrion Avenue. In later years the house itself was used as a residence for the boarders.

The seed of a religious vocation fell among the thorns of the anti-Catholic prejudice in which Inie grew up. But she continues in the same letter: 'The foreign mission field, work among pagans, or for that at home was the only real vocation I felt outside the one desire of my heart to live wholly and entirely for God.'

It was in China, years later, that Inie first met a Catholic priest in friendly conversation. It happened in the winter of 1892-3 when she was visiting a distant out-station and met a Spanish priest and his Chinese curate (see page 6). Possibly he told her that he was one of twenty Spanish Dominican priests working in Fujian Province, with the help of twelve Chinese priests.

In such a mountainous country with poor communications, the Protestant missionaries would have had little idea of the extent of the Catholic Mission with its twenty-four churches and thirty-nine schools. Also its glorious past reaching back to 1642 when Father Francis Fernandez landed in Fujian. Six years later he was captured, starved, and beaten to death, becoming the first of many Dominican martyrs in Fujian. 'The blood of martyrs is the seed of Christians'.

The Dominican priest whom Inie met was very probably Padre Miguel Vila, born 1860 in Catalonia.[68] He is remembered as 'one of the most illustrious missionaries in the latter part of the Dominican Mission in Fujian'. After his meeting with Inie he could write in a memoir in 1924 that he had not seen a European woman for thirty years, had not been to Foochow for thirty years, had not seen electric lights for thirty years, nor ever seen a car or aeroplane. He never left China and died still active in 1941.

It is no wonder that Inie recognized in him 'the embodiment of heroic self-denial'. But the admiration must have been mutual because at that time no Catholic woman religious was attempting or was allowed to take the risks these young Protestant women were taking in the service of God. Padre Vila's prayers would have supported Inie on her long road towards the Catholic faith.

So when St. Dominic welcomed him home in 1941, Inie also would surely have been there to thank him!

Notes

1 Although Mina is never mentioned as Jemima, her sister-in-law's name is given as Jemima and Mina in the Clergy Succession lists of the Diocese of Armagh. This would indicate that Mina is an accepted diminutive and would be pronounced MINE-a.

2 The name Inie would seem to be a diminutive. In the records of the Diocese of Armagh Mrs Newcombe's name is given as Elizabeth Maria Frances Wilhelmina. Her daughter always signed herself Inie Elizabeth. Her birth and baptism certificates have not been found. But in the entry for her religious profession in the register of the Carmelite Monastery she gives her mother's name as Inie Elizabeth Frances Maria Wilhelmina. This would seem to prove that she believed Inie to have been one of her mother's names and not a diminutive of Wilhelmina. (Possibly she was christened Wilhelmina and disliked it!) Inie was pronounced to rhyme with 'tiny', as it was confused with Irene in some of the sources.

3 Sister Mary Assumpta is the source. In the profession register her Catholic baptism is stated to be conditional and the date of her baptism at Drogheda is given.

4 All the information for this chapter is a weaving of Sister Winefride's recollection of the stories Inie herself told and the biographical notes on the family written by Flora Codrington, and based on conversations with the Newcombe sisters in China.

5 From the same sources as Chapter 2 except the excerpt from Inie's account of her conversion in 1928.

6 It is assumed that the children attended St Philip and St James Church, since it was nearer than All Saints on Carysfoot Road.

7 Again the excerpt in Inie's words is from her conversion account.

8 Letter to Father Cunningham, 19th July 1931.

9 Information supplied by the Dominican Sisters.

10 From the above-mentioned letter of 19th July 1931.

11 Quoted in *At the Eleventh Hour* as Inie's own words, probably remembered from a remark made as a Carmelite: 'Later she humorously said that as a Protestant she had had great faith in what she called the Fortieth Article, namely that the Church of Rome was a "sink of

iniquity".' In the original draft written by Mother Mary of Carmel, to this is added: 'The Romish Church was infra dig, something for the servants and simple peasants of the bogs'.

[12] From the records of the C. of I. Diocese of Armagh.

[13] the story is told by a friend with whom she lived and included in *The Eleventh Hour.*

[14] From the conversion account.

[15] From *the Garden of the Lord* by Edith Couch, page 3, kept with the CEZMS archives at Birmingham University.

[16] The river Min divides into two branches to form Nan Tai Island. The bridge to the island is in two sections divided by a footing on a small islet.

[17] Much of the information taken from Edith Couch is corroborated by Irene Barnes in her book *Behind the Great Wall*, 1896, reprinted by Frederiksen Press in 2007.

[18] Manuscript kept in Birmingham University Library, Special Sections.

[19] Nb. The seventy miles up river usually took five days because of the slow methods of travel: the scenery was wild and beautiful, the river alive with craft of many kinds, from tiny sampans to huge cumbersome rafts. Further upstream there were rapids and beautiful mountain scenery. The whole province is very mountainous.

[20] Edith Couch, p.35.

[21] Letter 1917, p.1V

[22] There is some confusion as to who was at Ciong Bau and for how long. Edith Couch seems to think Miss I. Newcombe was there 1889-1891 and with Miss Johnson was the first to enter Kieng Ning city. The Annual report for 1904 states that Hessie and Miss Johnson were the first, fourteen years previously, ie, in 1890. But Hessie was never stationed there and H. Newcombe would probably be a mistake for I. Newcombe. Irene Barnes writing in 1896, however, gives a very brief mention of the entry into the city in 1892 by Miss B. Newcombe and Miss Johnson. Mary Darley, writing in *Cameos of a Chinese City* in 1915, p.154, definitely states that it was Miss Inie Newcombe and Miss Johnson who stayed two days in the city in 1891.

[23] This letter is ascribed to Hessie in the Annual Report of 1892. In Edith Couch (p.38) it is ascribed to Hessie also but there is a correction in the margin in handwriting very similar to Inie's: '?Inie'.

[24] Edith Couch says on p.38 that Miss Johnson and Miss H. Newcombe rented the house at Ching Ho, but the H is crossed out and again corrected in the margin to 'I', in the same handwriting as mentioned above.

25 The Annual Report of 1893 says Benjamina was at Nang Wa.

26 The story of Mrs Ahok is given in Edith Couch, p.19 and in Irene Barnes, Chapter 6, p.60.

27 Edith Couch, p.26.

28 Letter to CEZ, 1917.

29 Edith Couch, p.27.

30 Sister Winefride's recollections.

31 From Miss Codrington's biographical notes.

32 Inie seems to restrict the term 'Protestant' to the sectarian version, the only one she had known. But on her return from Japan she attended church with Mina.

33 From the conversion account.

34 Ibid.

35 From the Roll of Missionaries Register (Book 1), CEZ archives, Birmingham University.

36 Annual Report, 1893.

37 Edith Couch, p.27.

38 Irene Barnes: *Behind the Great Wall* p.119.

39 Edith Couch, p.27 and Annual Report 1907 by Miss Burroughs.

40 *Behind the Great Wall*, p131, letter from Mrs Stewart, 1895.

41 Ibid, p.126 and the following account of the massacre..

42 Annual Reports 1895-1897.

43 Edith Couch, p.43.

44 Roll of Missionaries Register (Book 1).

45 Most of the information is taken from the Salvation Army publication: *All the World*, the mission bulletin; *God's Army*, by Cyril Barnes, 1978, Lyons Publishing; *Short History of the Japanese Mission*, by Captain Matilda Hatcher, 1952 typescript; various numbers of *War Cry*, both English and Japanese editions.

46 Letter to *All the World*, 1897.

47 Ibid.

48 All information from *All the World*.

49 It was published in *All the World*, May 1900.

50 Flora Codrington mentions the S.A. bonnet in her notes on the family.

51 Information taken from the English *War Cry* and *God's Army*.

52 Research on the Internet produced a passenger list of the SS Campania, arriving at New York from Cork on Feb.18, which includes Inie Newcombe, aged 46, from Dublin. The Salvation Army Heritage Centre

found the following in the *War Cry* of 21 January, 1905, p.10: 'Staff Captain Newcombe, who has been resting in this country is returning to her much-loved work in the Far East. The Staff Captain was one of the pioneer party who planted the Army Flag in Japan nine years ago.'
In the *War Cry* of 18 March, 1905 p.4, we find: 'Staff Captain Newcombe who helped pioneer our work in Japan, whither she is now returning, is conducting meetings in and around New York.'
At the end of March the 25th anniversary of the Army's arrival in USA was celebrated by a special Congress. But if Inie landed in Yokahoma on 3rd April, she would have left New York before it took place.

[53] Annual Reports.

[54] Edith Couch, p.65.

[55] The graves were at Foochow English Cemetary.

[56] According to the Roll of Missionaries Register, Benjamina sailed with her sister on 4th October, in the SS.Sardenia.

[57] The historical data in this chapter is taken from *Basic Intermediate History* by T.Stevin, p.90-97 (out of print).

[58] Lloyd George's ultimatum was: 'Acceptance or return to immediate and terrible war.'

[59] Canon Cronin, Parish Priest of Rathgar, church of the Three Patrons.

[60] Mother Lavery may even have authored the CTS pamphlet *At the Eleventh Hour*, from which these details are taken.

[61] Biographical details are from the obituary of Fr. Cunningham, in the Menevia Record, February 1954, and letters from the niece of Winefride Noonan, 5 April 2003.

[62] Originally named Central House, a wool store. When it became a hotel, it was for a time called Central Hotel.

[63] Inie has at last realised her mistaken spelling of Miss Noonan.

[64] She was photographed standing by the window of the priest's sacristy, showing the blocks of stone of which the old house was built.

[65] Thomas Ellis was a retired Judge of the Indian Rota and legal advisor to the Governor. He was known locally as Judge Ellis.

[66] This ceremony is now very different, as it is incorporated into the Mass for Solemn Profession of Vows.

[67] When the Annexe was further extended in 1957 it became difficult to distinguish the original layout of the ground floor. Thus it is quite possible that Inie's cell was what is now a corridor and store cupboards with no view, rather than the present Oratory.

[68] Information kindly supplied by the Dominican Archivists of Rome, Madrid and Manila.

Acknowledgements

This story has been pieced together from many sources, some of which were written during the life-time of the Newcombe sisters and whose authors are long since rejoicing with them in heaven. The letters of the four missionaries have nearly all been lost but were quoted in the following publications:

The Garden of the Lord by Edith Couch, about 1929, available in type-script from the CEZMS archives, Birmingham University Library;

Behind the Great Wall by Irene Barnes, 1896, reprinted 1992 by Dodo Press;

Robert and Louisa Stewart: In Life and Death by Mary Watson, 1896, reprinted 2010 by Dodo Press;

For His Sake: letters of Elsie Marshall 1896 reprinted;

Letters of Dr. James Gregory. Available on Internet search;

Nellie, Topsy and Annie: Australian martyrs. Paper written by Ian Welch 2004.

Thanks are due to the following archivists for invaluable help with the research:

Commissioner Karen Thompson of the Salvation Army Heritage Centre;

The Archivist of the Tokyo Salvation Army;

The Archivists of the Dominican Order at Rome, Madrid and Manila;

The Project Researcher, Special Collections, Birmingham University Library.

This book would never have seen the light without the support and encouragement of Sister Carmel Warde O.P.of the Sion Hill

Dominican convent whose nuns Inie could see from her bedroom window at Aunt Lily's house. Since 1998 Sister Carmel has given invaluable help with research, but her greatest contribution has been her moral support of the author- compiler, often over-awed by the sheer scope of the project and the holiness of those Victorian women missionaries.

Last but not least, my thanks are due to my Carmelite Sisters of Dolgellau whom I joined with five others when we were obliged to close our monastery in Birmingham in 1990, and not least to the Sister who for over a decade has guided and advised with unfailing patience, turning hand-written or typed pages into an expertly edited book.

To God be the Glory!